The Invisible Clash

FBI, Shin Bet, and the IRA's Struggle against Domestic War on Terror

by

DAVIS TRUMAN

Table of Contents

C H A P T E R   O N E

INTRODUCTION

Terrorism has existed as a form of warfare since prehistoric periods. Although it was not coined as an official term until the eighteenth century, the phenomenon is not new. If one may be so bold, Moses used a form of God-supported terrorism to break away from the Pharaoh of Egypt. Although some might disagree with this insight, since Moses was trying to do good, indeed, the Egyptians did not feel this way. Eventually, this form of terrorism was successful. The Assassins, a sect of the larger Ismaili sect of Muslims, developed a specific religious doctrine that justified the murder of their religious and political rivals. They were later suppressed by the Mongols. The Catholic church was not above using a form of religious terrorism during the Dark and Middle Ages, threatening hapless populations with a life in hell if they did not follow the church's tenants. They could manipulate, dominate and prosper by threats of excommunication and the Inquisition. The common thread of this form of terrorism is an effort at religious dominance. This brings to mind the definition of "terrorism." Although activities characterized as terrorism have escalated and declined with world situations, there is no precise or widely-accepted definition. This is made more difficult by the fact that the word "terrorism" has currently become a fad word applied liberally to various acts of violence that may not be terrorism Governments label violent acts committed by their political opponents as terrorism. At the same time, anti-government groups claim to be the victims of terrorism perpetrated by the government. The word "terrorism" depends on one's point of view and implies a moral judgment. If the label "terrorist" can be successfully applied by one party to its opponent, that party persuades the majority to adopt its moral viewpoint.

One of the myriad difficulties in defining "terrorism," "terrorist," or "terroristic" is the relativity of these concepts. This comes from differing perspectives and conflicting interests of those who have attempted to define terrorism. Also, there are intrinsic complications in reaching a neutral definition of a concept with ideologically solid and emotional implications. Terrorism may refer to actions primarily conducted to produce fear and alarm for various purposes. In general, however, it is frequently applied to similar acts of violence — ransom kidnappings, hijackings, sensational killings — in which the perpetrators may not intend to produce terror. Once a group acquires the label "terrorist," everything they do, whether planning to produce terror or not, becomes a terrorist act. If the group robs a bank or an arsenal, usually considered urban guerrilla tactics, these acts become terrorist acts. The difficulties in defining terrorism have resulted in the cliche that "one man's terrorist is another man's freedom fighter."

Terrorism is defined by the nature of the act, not by the perpetrators' identity or cause. All terrorist acts are crimes, but all crimes are not terrorist acts. Terrorist acts also would violate the rules of war if the state of war existed. These acts involve violence or the threat of violence coupled with specific demands, and the violence is directed mainly against civilian targets.

Political motives are the driving force behind the violence, and those actions are generated to garner maximum publicity. This definition is not restricted solely to nongovernmental groups. Sometimes governments with their armies and their secret police may also be terrorists. The threat of torture is a form of terrorism intended to create dread of the regime and obedience to authorities. Some scholars use terrorism to refer to nongovernmental groups, while the term "terror" applies to similar incidents carried out by the state. This distinction may be because while most nongovernmental acts of terror are international, state terrorism is internal. This does not rule out international incidents of state terrorism, such as the assassination of Trotsky. A stumbling block in defining terrorism, according to criminologist Grant Wardlaw, is a moral problem Attempts at definition are often based on the assumption that some types of political violence are justifiable while others are not. The latter is usually classed as terrorism, while the former is uncertain. Two examples of this uncertainty are the United States Air Force's secret bombing of Laos and Israel's preemptive strike against a nuclear reactor in Iraq in 1981.

The bombings of Laos were justified by the United States government originally because Pathet Lao forces shot down two "reconnaissance" aircraft. Later on, the bombing continued because communists from North Vietnam were assisting the Pathet Lao and bringing supplies into Laos via the Ho Chi Minh Trail. Targeting was tight, but it did not prevent civilian casualties and disruption. The Israelis were disturbed when they discovered the Iraqis had a nuclear development program. Although Iraq and Iran were engaged in conflict, the Israeli government believed that the nuclear program was aimed at their eventual destruction. They attempted to halt the progress of this program by appealing to France and the United States, but Iraq did not respond to this pressure. Prime Minister Menachem Begin realized that an airstrike would bring down condemnation from world governments and might even bring Iran and Iraq together. Still, he felt a preemptive move was the lesser of all evils. On June 7, 1981, the Israeli Air Force bombed the nuclear reactor at al-Tuweitha and completely destroyed it. One French technician and nine Iraqis were killed. Although the Pathet Lao and their communist supporters condemned the bombings, the United States government believed it was justified to maintain democratic freedom in Southeast Asia. In their view, the perceived ends justified the means. The Israelis believed the same, even in the face of world condemnation.

A definition must transcend behavioral descriptions, including individual motivation, social milieu, and political purpose. Unfortunately, this has been difficult in the past because scholars have found it easier to focus on behaviors and their effects rather than consider motives and politics. Academics find it difficult to communicate with policymakers and law enforcers because the latter cannot reconcile analytical techniques with the real world. This lack of reconciliation is seen as an inability to distinguish between "right" and "wrong" acts. Therefore, the definition should be based on moral justification; the proper study of terrorism should not justify the phenomenon. To understand the nature of terrorism, Wardlaw believes one must examine its relationship to other forms of civil, military, and political violence and criminal behavior. One of the central problems in defining terrorism lies with the subjective nature of terror. The use of terror does not necessarily have to be politically motivated. Many criminals increasingly resort to "terrorist" tactics for personal gain. Sociopathic individuals may terrorize due to their condition. Some members of society may be bored and frustrated with society and may terrorize to vent their rage or engage in symbolic acts of protest. Distinctions between these various forms of terrorism may be blurred because criminals or sociopaths who engage in terrorism may pretend to legitimate themselves by adopting political slogans and collaborating with official terrorist movements that often recruit them.

THE DEVELOPMENT OF TERRORISM

As mentioned previously, terrorism goes back to the development of prehistoric man. It is an outgrowth of guerrilla warfare, which may be the oldest form of warfare. Prehistoric people fought guerrilla to keep their neighbors on their toes. It was a matter of survival. Later this type of fighting became more organized as armies emerged and conventional warfare emerged. The terms "terrorism" and "terrorist" began in the French Revolution. Terrorism was defined in the Dictionnaire de la Academie Fran^aise as a system or regime of terror in 1798. Still, a French dictionary published in 1796 mentioned that the Jacobins or revolutionaries used the term positively when discussing their activities. Not long after, "terrorist" became an epithet with criminal implications. Since then, terrorism has represented almost every imaginable form of violence, although many may not follow the broad definitions discussed earlier.

After the French Revolution, terrorism found another niche later in the nineteenth century. It was used extensively by the Russian revolutionaries in 1878 - 1881 and by radical national groups in Ireland, Macedonia, Serbia, and Armenia. Anarchists in France, Italy, Spain, and the United States also embraced terrorism as a means to an end in 1890. In Russia, historically, one of the most essential terrorist movements was the Narodnaya Vofya, which operated between January 1878 and March 1881. This organization evolved a specific policy of terrorism and was responsible for a concerted terrorist campaign against the Tsar and his authority. According to one of their theoreticians, terrorism was considered a cost-effective form of struggle while ethically a superior choice to the mass carnage resulting from an insurrection. The difference between this terrorist campaign and the anarchist activities elsewhere in Europe was that Narodnaya Volya's terrorism was a directed campaign. In contrast, anarchist terror tended to be an individual activity.

Narodnaya Volya faded as a group, and with it, terrorism. The new wave of Russian terrorism surfaced in 1902 with the formation of the Social Revolutionary Party. Their theory for using terrorism was significantly different from previous terrorist campaigns. Instead of using terrorism as a solitary weapon to replace mass struggle, it was a tool to supplement and strengthen the masses' revolution. This new theory was more attractive to the populace, whereas the theory espoused by Narodnya Volya appealed to the intelligentsia. Although anarchists were also considered terrorists, there was a distinct difference between their ideology and the revolutionaries. Anarchists believed in destroying the prevailing social order because any state was exploitative. Violence and bloodshed were the only purgatives to cleanse society. Socialists, who used terrorism strictly as a tool, viewed the anarchists as fanatical and dangerous because they promulgated no concrete ideas for a future society.

Further deviation from socialist and anarchist dogma was the value of the proletariat. Socialists assigned the mission of overthrowing capitalism to the proletariat, while anarchists put their faith in peasants and thieves. In the anarchists' view, numbers willing to undertake acts of violence were primary to the vanguard. After the First World War, terrorism was at a standstill. No one was interested in social change because the war had wrought it. The depression set in and was followed by the Second World War. During this war, there were many technological advances in the military and civilian sectors; Mao Tse-tung exploded onto the scene, successfully, if not brutally, bringing communism to China. After the Second World War ended, the world was ripe for change. The United States and the Soviet Union had emerged as big winners and began to compete for hegemonic control of the world through military might. In the Middle East, Israel declared independence to establish a Jewish homeland as part of their covenant with God. Unfortunately, the Palestinians who lived there were unhappy about being displaced for a covenant not of their making.

The French pulled out of Vietnam after their embarrassing defeat at Dienbienphu, and the United States stepped in to advance their "domino theory" as their fear of communist domination increased with the establishment of East Germany, North Korea, and Cuba. Having decided that Asia was ready for democracy, United States policymakers ascertained that if Vietnam fell to communism, Asia would be under communist rule. Ho Chi Minn, leader of the Vietminh, began a guerrilla campaign against the

Americans, occasionally using terrorism as a form of psychological warfare. The Vietnam War inspired students to think of government in a whole new way. Although the victories won by the Allies in the Second World War had made democracy a popular form of government, these young people and some older socialists saw American efforts to push democracy in Vietnam as imperialist expansionism. It was their duty to expose this crime to the masses. Out of student protest groups grew the second generation of terrorists in Europe and the United States.

Protesters were particularly active in West Germany, where a group of left-wing, politically intellectual men and women organized underground publications and peaceful protests in sympathy with antiwar activists in the United States. The objective changed when the leader of the left-wing group, Rudi Dutschke, began to notice that the coalition government set up under the Marshall Plan had no opposition in the parliament. Dutschke questioned the coalition's legitimacy, stating that it was no less autocratic than the Nazi regime had been. In fact, some former members of the Nazi party had been retained to fill critical positions within the coalition.

This was intolerable to Dutschke, who took a radical, oppositional stance toward the government and confronted them with violence. He considered their idea of society inhuman and decadent and felt his behavior was justified. The anti-authoritarian student movement began to spread under the direction of Dutschke throughout Germany. By 1968, their actions began to reflect the revolutionary groups of the Third World, mainly because the violence against "dictatorship" and "terror from above" those groups used justified the students' violence against a democratic society. This student movement decided to base its revolution on a mixture of tenets espoused by Hegel, Marx, Lenin, Mao, Ho Chi Minh, Stokely Carmichael, Eldridge Cleaver, Che Guevara, and Jean-Paul Sartre. They all underlined this doctrine: "A guerrilla fighter slays his enemy. In that act of pure violence, there is a double act of liberation. The victim has been freed from his false role, and the victor has freed his own spirit for authentic manhood."

This dialectic solely concerned with life and death was meant to legitimize their violent actions. Meanwhile, in Italy, the Red Brigades were also formed in response to student and labor unrest of the late 1960s. Formerly activists in the Italian Communist Party, their objective was to educate, organize and encourage the working classes to throw off the oppressive rule of capitalism by an armed proletarian revolution. From the beginning, the Red Brigades were committed to using violence against the state to overthrow the Italian government, experiencing a political and economic crisis because the socialists in power could not develop effective coalitions. In contrast with international terrorist incidents in Western Europe and the Middle East, spectacular incidents rarely happened in the United States during the 1970s. The smaller incidents were not generally made known or publicized outside a small circle of policy, intelligence, and law-enforcement officials, so the general American public could ignore the problem.

During this decade, bombings were the most popular method for instituting terror within the United States. Since most of the terrorist groups were small and relatively unsophisticated, bombings were the simplest strategy because they required little technical expertise, little risk, and little organization. This accounted for bombings being the highest percentage of terrorist acts. From 1970 to 1980, there were four-hundred twenty-seven bombing incidents within the United States, which resulted in one-hundred-one deaths. Most of the domestic terrorist activities were carried out by three groups during the 1970s. The Weather Underground was responsible for forty-six bombings, including the Pentagon, the State Department, and the Capitol. In support of independence for Puerto Rico, the Fuerzas Armadas de Liberation National (FALN) accomplished fifty-eight bombings between 1975 and 1980. From 1974 to 1978, the New World Liberation Front (NWLF) carried out seventy bombings in the San Francisco Bay area.

Towards the end of the decade, terrorist incidents declined in the United States, which was attributed to the improved counterterrorism abilities of the Federal Bureau of Investigation (FBI). Although they acknowledged that domestic terrorism was far from being checked, the lack of terrorist activity during the 1980s changed the priorities of the FBI. Several theories have been advanced on why terrorism in the United States did not reach the tragic proportions exhibited in Western Europe and the Middle East. Colonel James B. Motley of the National Defense

University offered four reasons. First, the relative absence of political terrorism in the United States can be attributed to social and political "safety valves." Second, "terrorism is in the eye of the beholder " Perceptions of the severity of terrorism are based on spectacular acts, not statistics. Few terrorist incidents in the 1970s qualified as national media events. Third, foreign terrorists rarely operated on American soil during this time. The fourth reason may be the lack of lethality associated with terrorist incidents in the United States. Most of the bombings were directed against property, and with an average of eight deaths a year, this hardly seemed significant to the American public. From the brief history of terrorism cited here, it is evident that terrorism will continue to plague democracies as long as it remains effective. Have policymakers in the United States realized the seriousness of domestic and international groups perpetrating terrorism on American soil?

THE PURPOSE OF TERRORISM

The use of terror to introduce and exploit fear may serve several purposes. Depending on the situation, terrorism may be directed simultaneously at several strategic and tactical objectives. One of the principal aims of terrorism is to divide the population from the government and/or authority figures representing that government Success is guaranteed if the terrorists have low levels of actual political support but high potential for such support. If the potential is low, terrorism may be counterproductive, leading to mass outrage and hatred. It may also lead to counter-violence from vigilante groups or rival terrorist units. The original terrorists' actions will then be neutralized, making their influence on policy and/or constitutional changes ineffective. Fear and the psychology behind it is the primary road to success for terrorists. They must know the effects of disorientation and the nature of the society they are trying to affect. They must disorient the population by demonstrating the government's inability to provide security for them, including safety and order. More importantly, they must isolate citizens to prevent them from drawing strength from the usual social support, forcing them to depend upon their own resources. Thornton says, "Disorientation occurs when the victim does not know what he fears when the source of his fear lies outside his field of experience."

The results of instilling fear to produce personal disorientation can be unpredictable. First, political action, the goal of the terrorists, may not be provoked by fear. The populace may develop a psychological tolerance to violence, which can be a precursor to hostility. That ensuing hostility may be directed towards the terrorists or the government for their inability to provide security; this may be an unacceptable risk to the terrorist group. A second factor is the terrorist use of propaganda. The aim of this propaganda must be to tip the balance so that the government becomes the target for people's aggression. This is a delicate, difficult operation; many terrorist groups have failed and been destroyed due to their lack of finesse. Some terrorism theorists disagree over the extent to which the success of terrorism depends on the polarization of society. Terrorism will not result in long-term ideological support. The support given under coercion is unlikely to develop into a more enduring allegiance unless it can be systematically maintained over a long period. On the other hand, unconditional support of the populace is not necessary. All a terrorist campaign needs from a large proportion of the population is "non-denunciation" or malleability.

A goal of terrorist tactics related to community disorientation is provoking the government into invoking illegal or unconstitutional repressive measures or forcing intervention by a third party. The government uses illegal methods which deprive ordinary citizens of their human rights to suppress terrorists; they may lose legitimacy and public confidence and support. Carlos Marighela was quite specific about this method in his Mitrimatmal of the Urban Guerrilla. "The government can only intensify its repression, thus making the lives of its citizens harder than ever. Homes will be broken, police searches will be organized, innocent people will be arrested, and communications will be broken. Police terror will become the order of the day, and there will be more and more political murders." Publicity is also an aim of terrorism, sometimes the primary aim. By staging spectacular acts guaranteed to gain world attention, terrorists achieve recognition of their cause and project themselves as a force that must be reckoned with. Because terrorist groups are usually tiny, they must indulge in dramatic and shocking violence to be noticed. The media has become an important catalyst for expressing the terrorists' message. Terrorist activities have many ambitions. The primary aim is to create fear and gain concessions. They also strive to obtain maximum publicity for their cause, provoke repression, break down social order, and build morale in the movement. Their success depends on the accuracy of the terrorist calculations concerning timing, degree, and type of terrorist activities.

Terrorism will continue to have high and low activity; groups will form and dissolve. But the threat will always be present, waiting to strike at the most opportune instant. The termination of the cold war has brought some peace around the world, but the new way of warfare is a regional conflict. This is the perfect setting for terrorism. The United States had some dealings with domestic terrorism, as mentioned previously, but it seemed insignificant compared with international terrorism. The FBI handled those groups and eventually brought them down through tactics such as infiltration and slander. If any American lives were lost in terrorist incidents, they happened overseas, not on American soil. On 26 February 1993, the bombing of the World Trade Center brought Americans out of their fog of false security. The Atlantic Ocean was no longer a barrier to those who wanted to get to the United States and commit terrorist acts. On 19 April 1995, the bombing of the federal building in Oklahoma, which left one-hundred sixty-eight people dead, showed that domestic terrorists were alive and well. International terrorists were not the only danger to this country. Domestic terrorists did not have to be part of an organized group. Although tragic, it was sensational in its violence. It brought to the forefront the grievances of paramilitary and white supremacist groups who swore they had nothing to do with it but rode the wave of insecurity exhibited by the population. Although the FBI successfully apprehended the alleged perpetrators, the events had already occurred, and people died. In this book, we will explore the effectiveness of the FBI in countering terrorism that may escalate.

CHAPTER TWO

THE FBI AND COUNTERTERRORISM

Domestic counterterrorism in the United States has not been as troublesome as in other countries. This country has been fortunate because, in the past, it was geographically and economically difficult for international terrorists to operate successfully. Our fortunes changed in the 1990s with the World Trade Center and Oklahoma bombings. These events have catapulted the FBI into the media spotlight and have the public speculating whether or not the FBI is equipped to deal with the increased threat. In this chapter, I will examine the FBI's historical dealings with counterterrorism and their preparations for managing counterterrorism today.

HISTORY

The Federal Bureau of Investigation (FBI) is responsible for the investigation and, if possible, preventing domestic terrorist activities. This is a carryover from their early fight against gang crime and, later, their dubious successes with their Counterintelligence Program (COINTELPRO). Although these activities usually did not involve outsiders, J. Edgar Hoover, the first director, considered gangs', communists', and hate groups' endeavors a form of terrorism against the Federal government. The agency, now known as the FBI, was founded in 1908 when Attorney General Charles J Bonaparte appointed an unnamed force of Special Agents to be the investigative force of the United States Department of Justice. Before that time, the Department of Justice borrowed agents from the United States Secret Service to investigate violations of federal crime laws within its jurisdiction. This special agent force was named the Bureau of Justice in 1909 and, after several other name changes, became the Federal Bureau of Investigation in 1935.

During the early period of the FBI's existence, its agents investigated violations of some of the comparatively few federal criminal violations, such as bankruptcy fraud, antitrust crime, and neutrality violations. During the First World War, the Bureau was responsible for espionage, sabotage, sedition, and draft violations. The passage of the National Motor Vehicle Act in 1919 further broadened the Bureau's jurisdiction. After the enactment of prohibition in 1920, the Gangster Era began. Criminals engaged in kidnapping and bank robbery, which were not federal crimes then. This changed in 1932 with the passage of a federal kidnapping statute.

In 1934, numerous other criminal federal laws were passed, and Congress gave Special Agents the authority to make arrests and carry firearms. The FBI's size and jurisdiction during the Second World War increased. With the end of the war and the advent of the Atomic Age, the FBI began conducting background security investigations for the White House and other government agencies and internal security matters for the Executive Branch.

Civil rights and organized crime became significant concerns of the FBI in the 1960s, as did counterterrorism, white-collar crime, drugs, and violent crimes during the 1970s and 1980s. With the end of the cold war, the FBI now concentrates its investigative efforts on seven major programs: counterterrorism, drugs/organized crime, foreign counterintelligence, violent crimes, white-collar crime, applicant matters, and civil rights.

The FBI operates under guidelines issued in 1983 by Ronald Reagan's Attorney General, William French Smith. The Smith guidelines were modified by Gerald Ford's Attorney General Edward Levi in 1976. The Levi guidelines were criticized as being too restrictive and cumbersome. Although the Smith guidelines were developed to rectify the Levi guidelines, they have come under the same criticisms lodged against the Levi guidelines. The FBI's investigative mandate is the broadest of all federal law enforcement agencies. The FBI, therefore, has adopted a strategic approach that stresses long-term, complex investigations. The FBI's investigative philosophy also emphasizes close relations and information sharing with other federal, state, local, and foreign law enforcement and intelligence agencies. Many FBI investigations are conducted in concert with other law enforcement agencies or as part of joint task forces.

THE FBI AND COUNTERTERRORISM: THE EARLY YEARS

The FBI's first foray into domestic counterterrorism began with their domestic Counterintelligence Program (COINTELPRO), an ill-fated, tragic, unconstitutional, but highly successful effort. In 1936, President Franklin D. Roosevelt was monumentally concerned about the extremist political developments in Europe and Asia. He informed Hoover that he was worried that the influence of these fascists; and communist organizations would heavily influence extremist organizations in the United States. Hoover confirmed his fears, and Roosevelt immediately ordered him to set in motion the machinery necessary to gather intelligence information on domestic communist and fascist organizations. Hoover reminded FDR that it was unconstitutional to spy on American citizens, mainly when they were not engaged in illegal activities. It was not illegal for a U.S. citizen to be a member of a communist or fascist organization Under the FBI's Appropriations Act. However, they could undertake investigations of this type at the secretary of state's request without going through Congress. A few days after that meeting, Hoover, Roosevelt, and Secretary of State Cordell Hull met and set the stage for COINTELPRO. They could not foresee the havoc wrought in the coming years. At that time, Roosevelt was only interested in monitoring activities. Eventually, operations monitoring political expression would be expanded to include disruption.

Monitoring began with the Communist Party of the United States of America (CPUSA). The activity was vigorous, but by 1940, the United States entered the Second World War, and Hoover believed that extended operations were justified. Electronic surveillance, mail openings, and surreptitious entry became routine, and because of these added activities, the FBI's budget expanded to forty-five percent of the entire Justice Department. When the war ended, Hoover could not afford to lose such a large budget. Fate was with him because the Soviet Union had become the enemy of the United States, and a "cold war" began. By 1956, several events had become public, supporting Hoover's claims that the Communist Party was a threat and had to be neutralized. The Alger Hiss affair, the arrest and subsequent conviction of the Rosenbergs, the Korean War, the Soviet atomic bomb test, and the McCarthy hearings supported Hoover's pronouncement that communism was "a menace to the American way of life." At the 279th meeting of the National Security Council on March 8, 1956, Hoover received authorization for the operations that later came to be known as COINTELPRO.

The systematic destruction of the CPUSA began with the denial of communist infiltration into organizations such as the United Farm Workers and the National Organization for the Advancement of Colored People (NAACP). The obstruction of infiltration by communists into the NAACP and other civil rights organizations was a particular obsession with Hoover. Martin Luther King, Jr was Hoover's specific target, and he used COINTELPRO in a vigorous but futile effort to discredit King from 1957 until he died in 1968. COINTELPRO stepped up its destruction of the CPUSA by adding anonymous mailings and infiltrations to the repertoire of dirty tricks. The FBI would identify a member of the CPUSA and inform their employer or the media through letters written by concerned citizens. Infiltration was particularly successful, and by the time the Communist Party was debilitated, agents and informants were actually making party policy. When COINTELPRO began in 1956, the Communist Party in the United States had a membership of approximately 22,000. By 1971, the figure was down to three-thousand members, but many were passive, and others were FBI informants.

In 1964, three members of the Council Federated Organization, a civil rights group, were murdered by several Ku Klux Klan members near Meridian, Mississippi. The news that these workers were missing captured the country's attention and was very much in keeping with the Klan's intention to spread terror throughout the South. President Johnson felt that this terror and the apparent kidnapping of these workers were intolerable. The FBI knew about these events and contemplated instituting a COINTELPRO against the KKK. When Johnson gave the word, the FBI was ready and moved. After two months of gathering intelligence against the Klan, the Intelligence division recommended initiating a "hard-hitting closely supervised coordinated counterintelligence program to expose, disrupt, and otherwise neutralize the Ku Klux Klan and specified other hate groups." The techniques used were similar to those utilized against the Communist Party. One popular and successful approach involved sending anonymous or fictitious materials to Klan members. FBI informants operating within the Klan reported a dramatic impact on Klan morale. These mailings created distrust, spread rumors, and disrupted and neutralized Klan activities. One mailing method included a postcard featuring derogatory cartoons of KKK members with simple messages. These messages were effective and designed to play upon the Klan's greatest strength and secrecy.

Another successful strategy was the "snitch-jacket" technique, which created an impression, through various communications media, that a Klan member was actually a police informant. This created distrust and in-fighting. A well-placed letter to a Klansman's employer was humiliating to that individual and also a successful deterrent. Klan units were also heavily infiltrated by informants, which provided complete membership lists for those anonymous mailings and intimate information about members that would have usually been unobtainable. For example, an informant discovered that a Klan member was collecting one-hundred percent disability from the Veteran's Administration (VA) while running a small contracting business. The local field office contacted the VA and the Internal Revenue Service (IRS) with this information; the disability checks stopped immediately, and the IRS made this man's life miserable. He certainly had no time to participate in Klan activities.

Although these operations successfully broke the back of the Ku Klux Klan, some infiltrations compromised the FBI. Gary Rowe was an employed informant for the FBI, and because he rose very quickly in the Klan's hierarchy, his career ended abruptly on March 25, 1965. On that day, a civil rights rally occurred in Montgomery, Alabama. Three Klan members and Rowe were assigned to monitor and, if possible, cause disruption. As the men were driving through Selma, they noticed an out-of-state car driven by a white female with a black male passenger. Mrs. Viola Liuzzo was a civil rights volunteer transporting demonstrators from Montgomery to Selma.

The four men decided to follow Liuzzo's car as it headed toward Montgomery, intending to " get a black and a white together " Eventually, the Klan members and Rowe could move alongside Mrs Liuzzo's car. They rolled down their windows and fired into her car. She died instantly, but her passenger managed to keep the car under control and survived. Rowe maintained that he did not fire his weapon but had been an accessory to the crime. He became the star witness against the three Klansmen who were convicted. Because of this incident, President Johnson pressured Hoover to disrupt the Ku Klux Klan into oblivion. By 1968, the Ku Klux Klan was, for all practical purposes, decimated. Undercover informants like Gary Rowe participated in eighty-five percent of Klan actions. At one point, the FBI had so thoroughly infiltrated the Klan Hoover briefly considered installing an informant at the top of the organization to make Klan policy. When COINTELPRO ended, Klan membership had dropped from a high of 14,000 to four thousand. The murderous fury had been contained, but it was done at the expense of the Constitution. In successfully containing and neutralizing the Ku Klux Klan, the FBI violated constitutional liberties such as privacy and assembly.

The FBI did not limit its disruption methods to white hate groups. They targeted black nationalist hate groups as well. The incident that brought these groups to the forefront was an attempt by a motorcycle police officer to arrest a black man in Watts, a suburb of Los Angeles, for drunk driving. The man resisted, and an angry crowd gathered. Additional police contingents managed to keep the situation calm. Still, the next day, the Watts neighborhoods exploded into racial disorder of such magnitude that sixteen-thousand law enforcement personnel, including National Guardsmen, moved in to restore order. President Johnson was devastated that his "Great Society" seemed disintegrating and turned to the FBI for help. As it turned out, the FBI had been conducting microphonic surveillance on one black separatist group since 1960. It was effortless to increase its investigative powers to determine the origins and extent of the racial unrest.

After riots in Newark and Detroit in 1967, Johnson ordered the FBI to "search for evidence of conspiracy." The next COINTELPRO was developed against this backdrop, and the object was to "expose, disrupt, misdirect, discredit or otherwise neutralize the activities of black nationalist hate type organizations." To ensure the riots were reduced, Hoover continued increasing his Black Hate COINTELPRO among his field offices. The program seemed as successful as the one run against the Ku Klux Klan, but they underestimated the most dangerous group for unknown reasons.

The Black Panther Party was founded by Huey Newton and Bobby Seale, two college students in Oakland, in October 1966. Its purpose was to provide a unified black response to perceived police brutality in the Oakland area. Many blacks felt they were living in a colony ruled by white police. Panther members began to appear in public carrying weapons, but their first official action was directing traffic so that children could cross a busy street safely to get to school. They expanded their duties to include patrolling the crime-infested slums of Oakland, protesting rent evictions of African Americans, and counseling welfare recipients. They also monitored the actions of the Oakland Police Department and worked with African American prisoners. They stepped into the national arena when forty members boldly entered the California State Legislature fully armed, in battle dress to protest a bill that would outlaw carrying loaded weapons in public. They were all arrested, but they became a household word overnight. In October 1967, the Black Panthers collided head-on with Oakland police. Huey Newton and another Panther were stopped for a routine traffic violation. Newton got out of the car, and shooting erupted. Newton was shot four times but survived. One police officer was killed in the melee, and Newton went to prison. Despite the Panthers' propensity for violence and their growing national reputation, the FBI did not bother to target them in this new COINTELPRO.

Confrontations between the Panthers and the police increased, and still, the FBI did not react. The San Francisco field office resisted including them in COINTELPRO because the field agents did not think the tactics would be effective. Eventually, because of the tremendous news coverage devoted to the Panthers, FBI headquarters overruled this decision. The public wanted to know what the FBI was doing about these threatening exploits, and the FBI had no choice but to include them in the COINTELPRO target list. By 1968, Hoover described the Panthers as "the greatest threat to the internal security of this country." As mentioned previously, the number one goal of this COINTELPRO was to prevent the unification of black hate groups. Consolidation seemed to be Hoover's greatest fear. Goal three called for avoiding violence, but most COINTELPRO actions achieved the opposite result. In fact, this COINTELPRO generated the most violence of any run by the FBI. By 1971, when all the COINTELPROs ended, the Black Panthers had been decimated due to violent death, exile, and arrest. COINTELPRO came to an ignominious and explosive end when a small group of burglars broke into an FBI field office in a Philadelphia suburb and stole one-thousand documents detailing the FBI's domestic intelligence operations within the United States. The burglars, calling themselves the Citizens' Commission to Investigate the FBI, felt these covert operations were reprehensible and useless in a democratic society. They believed they were justified in committing a crime to expose a crime.

When Hoover was finally informed of this break-in, he was livid. The sacred walls of the FBI had been breached, and classified documents had been professionally stolen by an unknown group. He mounted the largest investigation to discover the identity of the perpetrators, but they were never apprehended. The documents were distributed to every major newspaper in the United States, but at the request of Attorney General Mitchell, The New York Times and the Los Angeles Times refrained from printing the documents. However, The Washington Post deemed this a "significant matter of public controversy" and went ahead with the story. This was the darkest period in the existence of the FBI.

In the late 1960s, the military worked closely with state and local police and National Guard units to coordinate scenarios for implementing martial law. Senator Sam Ervin's Constitutional Rights Subcommittee discovered a master plan called Garden Plot which was too unspecific to concern Ervin. Several years later, a freelance journalist uncovered a sub-plan of Garden Plot called Cable Splicer, which involved the Sixth Army. Cable Splicer was developed in a series of California meetings from 1968 to 1972, involving Sixth Army, the Pentagon, National Guard generals, police chiefs, sheriffs, military intelligence officers, defense contractors, and telephone and utility company executives. The participants played war games using scenarios that began with racial, student, and labor unrest and ended with the army being called in to bail out the National Guard, usually sweeping the area to confiscate private weapons and round up likely troublemakers. These games were conducted in secret, with the military personnel dressed in civilian clothes and arriving in nonmilitary transportation.

The United States Army's Counterintelligence Analysis Branch compiled organizational files, personality files, mug books, and "black lists," resulting in more than 117,000 documents. There were other filing systems in different locations maintained by other elements of the military intelligence bureaucracy. The United States Army Intelligence Command (USAINTC) had a network of fifteen-hundred agents stationed in over three hundred posts scattered throughout the country. These posts were stocked with communications equipment, tape recorders, cameras, lock-picking kits, lie detectors, and interview rooms with two-way mirrors. They also had direct lines to local police departments, teletype machines to field intelligence units, situation maps, closed-circuit television, and secure radio links. A one-hundred-eighty-man command center was created in 1968 after the assassination of Martin Luther King and the riots that followed. Its primary targets were colleges and universities. The Ervin subcommittee reported that military intelligence groups conducted offensive operations against anti-war and student groups, but the Pentagon refused to declassify the relevant records. Presumably, they never reached the intensity of the FBI's COINTELPRO. When USATNTC's domestic surveillance activities were publicly disclosed in the early 1970s, public anger and political reaction caused the command's activities to be sharply curtailed. In 1974, USAINTC ceased to be a major Army command. This was clearly a violation of the Posse Comitatus Act.

THE FBI AND COUNTERTERRORISM TODAY

The FBI, as the lead Federal law enforcement agency in the fight against terrorism, defines terrorism as "the unlawful use of force or violence against persons or property to intimidate or coerce a government, the civilian population, or any segment thereof, in furtherance of political or social objectives." The FBI's counterterrorism mission is to identify and neutralize the threat in the United States posed by terrorists and their supporters, whether nations, groups, or individuals. The FBI categorizes terrorism as domestic or international depending on the origin, base, and objectives of the terrorist organization/individual Domestic terrorism comes under the FBI's auspices. Acts constituting terrorism include terroristic assassination, hijacking, kidnapping, hostage-holding, bombing, arson, armed attack, and extortion. Because significant acts of terrorism violate state and federal law, concurrent criminal jurisdiction is the rule. Accordingly, the federal government can either act or defer to state jurisdiction and action depending on the incident's nature and local authorities' capabilities to deal with it. Appropriate federal law-enforcement assistance and support will be rendered upon request if local authorities are in charge.

The initial tactical response to a terrorist incident is made by the FBI Special Agent in Charge (SAC) at the scene. In describing the FBI's capabilities for responding to a domestic terrorist incident, former Deputy Attorney General Benjamin R Civiletti assured Congress that "the government's capabilities to meet the kinds of terrorist acts likely to occur inside the United States are sound and sufficient." He also believed that "the plans and procedures for meeting and effectively handling such incidents do not involve any infringement, dilution, or disregard of civil and Constitutional rights " The FBI possesses a wide range of capabilities to deal with possible domestic terrorism. Each FBI office and headquarters has contingency plans that are effective when a terrorist incident occurs. Such plans are the cornerstone of all other responses or actions. They include, for example, the chain of command, communications both within and outside the FBI, and the availability of specialized equipment and personnel. In cases involving hostage negotiations, teams of trained and experienced psychologists are available to provide on-the-scene psychological terrorist profiles and analyses to FBI hostage negotiators. The knowledge and experience such teams gain is shared with local law enforcement agencies through training sessions.

Another asset that equips the FBI to respond to terrorist acts is the Special Operations and Research Unit (SOAR). This group of FBI special agents is trained in psychology and criminology. The function of the SOAR unit is to accumulate and analyze facts about terrorist incidents and, through papers, articles, seminars, and training sessions, to pass on to other law-enforcement bodies guidance on dealing with terrorism. International terrorists operating in the United States are considered hostile foreign agents and are investigated under the Attorney General Guidelines for Foreign Intelligence Collection and Foreign Counterintelligence Investigations. These investigations are the responsibility of the FBI's Intelligence Division. Domestic terrorist groups originating in the United States are investigated under the Attorney General guidelines on General Crime, Racketeering Enterprise, and Domestic

Security/Terrorism investigations Investigations of domestic terrorism are conducted under the Domestic Terrorism Subprogram of the Criminal Investigative Division's Violent Crimes and Major Offenders Program.

The Counterterrorism Program (CTP) is responsible for preventing, hindering, and investigating the violent acts and criminal manifestations of terrorist groups and individuals involved in terrorism and related activities. Therefore, the CTP activities can be broken down into two primary areas: (1) the prevention of terrorism through the timely development of intelligence which is augmented by an exchange of information between the FBI and other agencies, both in this country and abroad, and (2) reaction to terrorist activity through criminal/counterterrorism investigations and other law enforcement options designed to arrest and convict terrorist groups' members and individuals who perpetrate other criminal acts related to terrorist activities Counterterrorism investigations are undertaken to detect, prevent, and/or react to unlawful, violent activities of individuals o; groups whose intent is to overthrow the government; interfere with the activities of a foreign government in the United States, substantially impair the functioning of the Federal Government, a state government, or interstate commerce; or deprive Americans or their civil rights as guaranteed by the Constitution, laws, and treaties ofthe United States. These criminal acts include violating the Protection of Foreign Officials, Neutrality, Extortion statutes, and firearms and explosives laws. Also, as a result of the passage of the Comprehensive Crime Control Act of 1984 (Title 18, USC, Section 1203, entitled "Hostage Taking"), the FBI acquired jurisdiction and authority to act, where appropriate, in certain terrorist-related hostage situations both within this nation and internationally.

Although the recorded number of actual terrorist incidents and terrorist incidents prevented in the United States has generally declined, this favorable trend should not be regarded as a signal that eradicating violent terrorism is close at hand. More properly, the reduction in terrorist incidents in the United States closely corresponds to the FBI's acceleration of an all-out counterterrorist effort characterized by the steady commitment of resources, enhanced counterterrorism training, and more efficient use of an increasingly effective intelligence base. The success of the FBI in this regard is even more evident when the rather few incidents of terrorism in the United States are compared against the number committed worldwide. The FBI has therefore concluded that any relaxation in their current efforts to counter terrorist activities within the United States could be detected by terrorists and may result in a reversal of what has otherwise been a sustained downturn in violent terrorist activity. The FBI is committed to a program of intensified investigative activity which will (hopefully) continue to successfully counter the violent intentions of terrorist organizations deployed in the United States. The arrest, prosecution, and incarceration of key leadership elements of various terrorist organizations, coupled with successful preventive measures, has significantly contributed to the decline in the number of terrorist incidents committed in the United States. It would, however, be incorrect to conclude that counterterrorism has been permanently eradicated.

The United States, because of its size, porous borders, open society, and official involvement in the global political arena, is constantly vulnerable to terrorist attacks in the United States in response to U.S. foreign policy initiatives or out of a desire to neutralize dissident behavior which may appear in emigre communities. Terrorist attacks by domestic terrorist groups also continue to occur because perceived social and political conditions have not changed to their satisfaction. Therefore, the FBI must maintain its aggressive counterterrorism initiatives at home and abroad. In any given year, the FBI conducts approximately two dozen full domestic terrorism investigations. Over the years since the Smith guidelines were adopted, nearly two-thirds of these full investigations were opened before a crime had been committed. The FBI has investigated right-wing, anti-government, anti-tax, paramilitary, and militia groups under this authority. They have been successful in preventing terrorist acts before they occurred. In 1993, for example, the FBI arrested several skinheads in Los Angeles after a lengthy investigation determined that they had been discussing and planning attacks on an African American church, Jewish targets, and other religious targets. On February 26, 1993, a massive explosion occurred in the garage beneath the Vista Hotel at the

World Trade Center complex in New York City. The bomb that caused the explosion consisted of approximately twelve-hundred pounds of explosives, making it one of the giant homemade bombs ever seen in the United States. Six persons were killed, and about one thousand were injured due to the attack.

Four of the six defendants indicted were convicted on all thirty-eight counts against them, including conspiracy to bomb targets in the United States, the bombing of the World Trade Center, and the use of explosive devices. They were each sentenced to two hundred forty years in prison and fined. A raid on a North Wildwood, New Jersey hotel by FBI Agents and local law enforcement officers on July 22, 1993, resulted in the arrest of Matarawy Mohammed Said Saleh. He was charged with conspiracy to bomb several sites in New York City. The group, of which he was a part, had targeted the headquarters of the United Nations, the federal building which houses the New York FBI office, the Lincoln and Holland tunnels, Egyptian President Mubarak during his 1993 visit to New York, and at least two U.S. political figures In 1994, the FBI scored a coup against the Abu Nidal organization in the United States Three men were apprehended and subsequently pled guilty to conspiring to participate in a terrorist organization. This group smuggled, transferred, and transported currency, information, and intelligence to other members of the Abu Nidal organization and worldwide. This group also obstructed investigations, fraudulently obtained passports for the members, bought weapons, and collected intelligence information.

In terms of domestic terrorism, two persons on the top ten fugitive list surrendered to the FBI in Chicago on December 6, 1994; Claude Daniel Marks and Donna Jean Willmott had been sought for eight years for assisting in an escape plan to liberate Oscar Lopez from the United States Penitentiary at Leavenworth, Kansas Lopez is a leader of the Armed Forces of National Liberation (FALN), a clandestine Puerto Rican terrorist group based in the continental United States. Since 1974, the FALN has been responsible for causing five deaths, eighty-four injuries, and over $35 million in property damages. A new development concerning terrorism within the United States has been the emergence of International Radical Terrorism (IRT). IRT may be defined as any extremist movement or group that is international and conducts acts of crime or terrorism under the banner of personal beliefs in furtherance of political, social, economic, or other objectives. The FBI believes that with continuing state sponsorship of international terrorism, IRT poses a significant threat to U.S. national security. The ever-present threat posed by state sponsors of terrorism to U.S. interests cannot be discounted. These nation-states continue to use violence and fear to bring about their demands. In fact, the phenomena of IRT continue to flourish, partly due to the support provided by sovereign states such as Iran and Sudan. Changing world conditions have also affected domestic terrorism within the United States. The threat of terrorism increases as changes occur within global politics, which could have an undesirable effect on terrorists or their supporters. Within the 1990 through 1994 time frame, events such as the ongoing Middle East peace process, the Provisional Irish Republican Army (PIRA) cease-fire agreement with the British Government, and the fall of the Soviet Union profoundly affected terrorism.

Should the cease-fire agreement between PIRA and the British Government hold or lead to further peace initiatives, this could radically change the face of terrorism in Great Britain and impact the United States, where many supporters of PIRA have been known to solicit funds and attempt to procure weapons to support PIRA's goals Further, terrorists who once enjoyed financial support from some former Soviet-Bloc states are now on their own with the collapse of the Warsaw Pact. Other political changes in global politics may also lead to a greater terrorist threat in the United States. Since the beginning of the historic Middle East peace talks in October 1991, Palestinian terrorist groups, Israeli right-wing organizations, and radical Middle East governments which oppose these negotiations have threatened to derail the peace dialogues. These "rejectionists" have threatened to use any means, including violence, to impede peace. The threat posed to the United States, which has taken the lead in this peace initiative, is ever-present.

FBI SOLUTIONS

For the most part, U.S. law enforcement initiatives have been somewhat successful at deterring individuals or groups engaged in terrorist activity from committing acts of terrorism against U.S. interests. Within the past five years, the U.S. counterterrorism response has successfully taken an aggressive approach to the problem of terrorism. Through this heightened proactive response, the FBI aggressively undertakes to identify and prevent the activities of terrorists before they strike. This preventative phase involves acquiring, through legal means, intelligence information related to groups or individuals who would choose terrorism to threaten or attack Americans, U.S. interests, or foreign nationals within the United States.

The information acquired is carefully analyzed, appropriately disseminated, and effectively used to prevent terrorist acts before they occur. The 1993 arrests of the New York City bomb conspirators demonstrate this proactive approach's effectiveness. A potentially devastating series of bombings was averted. US law enforcement agencies are unable to prevent all acts of terrorism. When terrorist acts do unfortunately occur, the FBI and other law enforcement agencies engage in effective investigations, resulting in successful criminal prosecutions. Successes such as the World Trade Center bombing investigation, which culminated in arrests, convictions, and imprisonment, and the Oklahoma investigation send a signal to would-be terrorists that the United States is a hostile environment for terrorists and that individuals willing to engage in criminal activities of this nature will not be tolerated. In addition to law enforcement initiatives, past success in the US. The government's battle to eradicate the terrorist threat can be attributed, in large part, to a joint counterterrorism effort among U.S. law enforcement agencies, luck, and two oceans. This coordinated effort has led to the formation of joint terrorism task forces. Increased cooperation among U.S. government agencies and departments with counterterrorism responsibilities has also led to greater information sharing.

An example of law enforcement agencies working together can be found in Texas. Several agencies in the central Texas region have joined together in a cooperative effort to address domestic terrorism. The Central Texas Counterterrorism Working Group (CTWG) represents a proactive effort to respond to the threat of terrorism in an area of the United States brimming with strategic commercial sites and critical military installations. Past terrorist activity in the central Texas region demonstrates the need for a coordinated approach to counterterrorism. For years, the region served as the base of operations and support for several domestic terrorism groups. These ranged from right-wing, white supremacist groups to left-wing cells, such as the May 19 Communist Organization (M19CO). Several cases have illustrated the belief among terrorists that the Central Texas region represents a safe haven from apprehension. One case involved Richard Scutari, head of security for the white supremacist group, the order and one of the FBI's Top Ten Most Wanted fugitives for his part in the June 1983 murder of a talk show host in Denver, Colorado After the slaying, Scutari fled Colorado for central Texas, where fellow white supremacists provided him refuge. His subsequent capture in San Antonio, Texas, demonstrated the area's attraction to domestic terrorists.

Members of the violent May 19 Communist Organization (M19CO) remain active. The group's affiliation with the central Texas region dates back to the turbulent 1960s when it operated freely among the less organized elements of the antiwar anti-establishment movement. While these movements declined as the Vietnam War drew close, M19CO diversified into domestic terrorism and directly assisted in staging a series of criminal acts, ranging from armored car robbery and murder to the November 1983 bombing of the U.S. Capitol Building in Washington, DC. Of the seven individuals responsible for the Capitol bombing, three were from Austin, Texas, and affiliated with M19CO's Austin cell. This cell was responsible for thefts of high explosives from the central Texas region. These explosives were ultimately used in the bombings in Washington, DC, New York City, and sites throughout the nation's northeast. Many M19CO members continue to live in the central Texas region and could conceivably provide support to other members. The Central Texas Counterterrorism Working Group was initially formed in 1987 as a joint project by the San Antonio Office of the FBI, the Texas Department of Public Safety, and the Texas Railroad Commission to identify terrorist groups, activities, and potential targets of opportunity in the central region of Texas. This group comprises forty-six law enforcement agencies representing Federal, State, and local levels of jurisdiction. These agencies range from local metropolitan police departments and county sheriff's offices to the State's Department of Public Safety, the Texas Ranger Service, and the FBI.

During the eight years of this group's existence, they have met bimonthly in those locations that may provide targets of opportunity, such as nuclear power plants and military installations. In addition to these meetings, the FBI has hosted joint training seminars focused on international terrorism, with guest speakers ranging from the Israeli government and academic officials to leaders of Islamic mosques. These seminars have also addressed domestic terrorism, primarily focusing on right-wing, white supremacist groups. These particular seminars have included speakers from undercover officers and case agents to the Grand Dragon of the Texas Knights of the Ku Klux Klan. The Central Texas Counterterrorism Working Group, grew out of a need to provide proactive counterterrorist security to a particularly vulnerable region of the nation. The key to its success is the high degree of cooperation among the group's members as they share information and expertise to enhance the security of the entire region. This concept of informed preparedness could form the basis for similar interagency counterterrorism working groups in other areas of the nation. Legislative initiatives have greatly aided the FBI in its counterterrorism mission. Congress has played a vital role in this success by providing appropriate legal tools, particularly legislation entitled the Comprehensive Crime Control Act of 1984 and the Omnibus Diplomatic Security and Antiterrorism Act of 1986. These acts greatly expanded FBI jurisdiction to include investigating terrorist acts abroad. More recently, the Aviation Security Improvement Act of 1990 has resulted in security enhancements at U.S. airports to ensure the safety of domestic air transportation systems. This act also provided a greater cooperative effort between the FBI and the Federal Aviation Administration.

Many members of international terrorist groups are reluctant to carry out an attack in the United States. This reluctance may be due, in part, to the fear of jeopardizing their current immigration status; fundraising capabilities; recruitment opportunities, propaganda activities to support their cause; and freedom of assembly within the United States. Many of the individuals who are members of international terrorist groups are fleeing crackdowns from their home governments and have sought the safe haven or refuge which is available to immigrants and asylum seekers here in the United States.

They live in freedom in the United States and continue supporting their cause, which may entail using propaganda to attract new members or supporters of their cause. Should they commit a violent act in which persons are injured or killed or property destroyed, they might alienate themselves and gain disfavor from individuals they are attempting to attract to their cause. Should they lose public sympathy or support, then they also stand to lose the financial support upon which they may have come to rely heavily. There has been a decrease in Puerto Rican terrorism. In the past, Puerto Rican terrorist groups struggling for Puerto Rico's independence from the United States have been responsible for most terrorist incidents perpetrated by domestic terrorist groups within the United States. During the last five years, the number of incidents committed by Puerto Rican terrorist groups has steadily declined. In 1990, five terrorist acts were committed by Puerto Rican terrorist groups in the United States and Puerto Rico; in 1991, the number of incidents decreased yet again to four. In 1992, the number of incidents decreased to one act of terrorism. During 1993 and 1994, no acts of terrorism were committed by Puerto Rican terrorist groups. This apparent decrease may be due, in part, to the November 1993 political referendum held in Puerto Rico in which a plurality of Puerto Ricans voted to maintain their commonwealth status. The results of this referendum appear to have deflated the independence movement of Puerto Rican nationalists, of whom only a minimal but militant faction condones the use of terrorism as the primary method of operation.

The threat posed by other terrorist groups has remained constant. During the past five years, there have been twelve incidents of terrorism associated with groups such as the Animal Liberation Front, Up the IRS, and the Earth Night Action Group. These groups, loosely defined as "special interest" terrorist groups, seek specific issue resolutions rather than widespread political changes. While the causes they promote may not be criminal, the means they use, violence and destruction, to attain their goals are. These individuals differ from traditional law-abiding special interest groups by using criminal activity and violence to achieve their goals. The FBI also defines other acts of criminal violence as acts of terrorism. Violent attacks perpetrated against abortion clinics and their personnel may, in fact, be terrorist-related. As a result, of the recent acts of violence targeted at abortion clinics, the Attorney General directed that the Department of Justice Task Force on Violence Against Abortion Providers be formed to actively investigate a possible criminal conspiracy to commit acts of violence against abortion doctors and/or their clinics. The FBI is part of this Task Force, comprised of the Bureau of Alcohol, Tobacco, and Firearms, the US Marshals Service, and criminal and civil rights attorneys from the Department of Justice.

The Attorney General Guidelines (AGG) states that a domestic security/terrorism investigation may be initiated when facts or circumstances reasonably indicate that two or more persons are engaged in an enterprise to further political or social goals wholly or in part through activities that involve force or violence and a violation of the criminal laws of the United States. f:iven this narrow definition b the AGG, most abortion-related investigations are not classifiable as "terrorist incidents" In many incidents, the perpetrator(s) are not identified. However, when the investigation reveals that two or more individuals are conspiring, the investigation is, at that point, reclassified as a domestic terrorism case and is then investigated by the task force. Although the FBI is examining abortion clinic crimes to determine their status as terrorists, some pro-choice individuals consider those actions as terroristic whether or not they follow the Attorney General's Guidelines. Historical parallels have been drawn between anti-abortionists and opposers of civil rights. African American voters were harassed, as were those women seeking legal abortions. The legislation made it more difficult for African Americans to vote; attempts have been made to overturn Roe v. Wade. Some African Americans were lynched or shot for being "uppity" because they continued to seek their rights; patients at abortion clinics were harassed. Houses owned by African Americans and churches they attended were bombed indiscriminately, as were the abortion clinics.

This harassment was allowed to continue until the Federal government realized that establishing a civil rights law was not a guarantee that civil rights would be granted. They sent in the National Guard to protect African Americans at the polls and passed stronger laws so that African Americans could vote safely. Before this happened, the Federal government ignored the situation or said it was a local issue. Pro-choice individuals also believe that until the anti-abortion groups organized under banners such as Operation Rescue, these terrorist tactics did not exist. As with the Ku Klux Klan, these groups spout rhetoric that incites fringe members to heinous actions; money flows into these groups, but no one knows from where; some of these groups are supported by religious organizations who disavow any knowledge when violence occurs; and these groups tend to argue and operate based on fear and emotion. Terrorist groups categorized as "right-wing" are defined as racist, anti-Semitic and are for the advancement of the white race. In addition to advocating white supremacy and hatred of non-white races, these groups have also engaged in acts of provocation and assault against federal and state law enforcement officials. Groups such as Aryan Nations, the Order, and Posse Comitatus fall into this category. The most significant instances of right-wing terrorism during the last five years occurred in July 1993, when members of the American Front Skinheads attempted to bomb the National Association for the Advancement ofColored People headquarters in Tacoma, Washington The bombing of the Oklahoma City federal building in April 1995 and the derailment of the Amtrak train in Arizona in August 1995 was allegedly committed by individuals who may have been associated with paramilitary right-wing groups.

Left-wing domestic terrorism is usually defined as being Marxist-Leninist in orientation. Groups such as the African National Jammu, the Dar-11 I Movement, and the Amaru Allah Community are defined as being leftist in their direction. Many Puerto Rican terrorist groups, such as the Armed Forces of National

Liberation and the Macheteros, also fall into this category. Left-wing terrorism has declined over the past five years, possibly due to the many arrests of leftist group leaders during the 1980s. Bands of right-wing militants, most calling themselves "militias," are becoming an increasing concern to the FBI. Although they have no centralized structure, there are linkages among some of them, sharing propaganda materials and speakers. The aims of these militias, often stated bellicosely, involve laying the groundwork for massive resistance to the federal government and its law enforcement agencies, as well as opposition to gun control laws.

According to the adherents, America's government is the main enemy (among others), constantly increasing authoritarian control and contemplating warfare against unsuspecting American citizens. Gun control legislation is the central strategy in a secret government conspiracy to disarm and control the American people and abolish their Constitutional "right to bear arms." The fear of government confiscation of their weapons is a paramount concern. Although gun control is the primary concern of most militias, there is also a movement to turn back the clock on federal involvement in other issues such as education, abortion, and the environment. Some leaders are also known as racists, religious bigots, and/or political extremists. Some northwest militia groups, for example, militia leaders with backgrounds in the Aryan Nations movement, Neo-Nazi groups, and the Ku Klux Klan. The Anti-Defamation League has found active militias in no fewer than thirteen states. Even though these militias seem primarily concerned with gun control, racist and anti-Semitic dialogue grows increasingly. Beginning in May 1978, a series of bombing incidents occurred across the United States for which there is no apparent explanation or motive. No person or group has been identified as the perpetrator(s) of these incidents.

The explosions have taken place in eight states from Connecticut to California, and, as a result of these bombings, three individuals have been killed and twenty-three injured. Between 1987 and 1993, these bombings stopped, but that changed in June 1993 when a well-known geneticist in California and a renowned computer scientist at Yale University opened packages that had been mailed to them and were severely injured by the explosions that resulted

Eighteen months later an advertising executive was killed in New Jersey followed by another explosion that killed a timber industry lobbyist in Sacramento, California on 24 April 1995. The perpetrator(s) are still at large as of this date.

On February 10, 1995, a counterterrorism bill drafted by the Clinton Administration was introduced in the Senate and the House of Representatives. There has been opposition to this bill based on several issues. Some senators and representatives believe that this legislation would:

1. 1 Authorize the Justice Department (the FBI) to pick and choose crimes to investigate and prosecute based on political beliefs and associations.
2. Repeal the provision barring the U.S. military from civilian law enforcement.
3. Expand a pre-trial detention scheme that puts the burden of proof on the accused.
4. Loosen the carefully-crafted rules governing federal wiretaps in violation of the Fourth Amendment.

5. Establish special courts that would use secret evidence to order the deportation of persons convicted of no crimes in violation of basic principles of due process.

6. Permit permanent detention by the Attorney General of aliens convicted of crimes, with no judicial review.

7. Give the President unreviewable power to criminalize fundraising for lawful activities associated with unpopular causes.

8. Renege on the Administration's approval in the last Congress of a provision to ensure that the FBI would not investigate based on First Amendment activities.

9. Resurrect the McCarran Walter Act's discredited ideological visa denial provisions to bar foreign speakers.

In the wake of the Oklahoma bombing, the Administration has pressed Congress to pass the counterterrorism bill, but reluctance is still prominent. Despite this opposition, The New York Times reported that the FBI recently proposed a national wiretapping system allowing law enforcement officials to monitor one of every one-hundred telephone lines in high-crime areas. Privacy rights advocates oppose this proposal, stating that this surveillance ability would far exceed the current needs of law enforcement officials nationwide. In recent years, these officials have conducted an annual average of less than eight-hundred-fifty court-authorized wiretaps or fewer than one in every 174,000 telephone lines. This plan would require Congressional approval (unlikely) and a court warrant to conduct the wiretaps. Privacy rights advocates fear a Big Brother surveillance capability might encourage law enforcement officials to use wiretapping much more frequently as an investigative tool. In a letter to Congressman Henry Hyde, the chairman of the Committee on the Judiciary, Louis Freeh, the FBI director, refuted this report. He reiterated that Congress did not expand the FBI's authority to conduct wiretaps, nor did the FBI ask Congress to do so.

The new law requires the FBI, on behalf of all law enforcement, to work with the telephone industry to identify technical design requirements for the industry to build into their systems. The FBI has not asked for the ability to monitor one out of every one-hundred telephone lines because it would be impossible to obtain that many court orders. Other FBI officials have asserted that the FBI is severely restricted in infiltrating known extremist groups, has no terrorism database like the Central Intelligence Agency's, and is powerless to stop extremist groups from masquerading as "religious groups." All of these claims are incorrect. The Smith guidelines, mentioned previously, make it clear that the FBI does not have to wait for blood in the streets before investigating a terrorist group. The guidelines expressly state: "In its efforts to anticipate or prevent crimes, the FBI must at times initiate investigations in advance of criminal conduct."

TRENDS

The lack of domestic terrorist activity until 1995 can be explained as a response to world events. Puerto Rican terrorism is dormant due to the political plebiscite in which Puerto Ricans voted to remain a commonwealth. This vote took the impetus out of the FALN's terrorist campaign for independence. Particular interest terrorist groups, including violent arms of environmental and animal rights activists, threaten U.S. interests. Criminal acts perpetrated against abortion service providers are currently being investigated by a DOJ Task Force to determine whether a conspiracy exists. Several international terrorist groups continue to maintain or increase their presence in the United States. These groups continue infiltrating their members into the country via legal and illegal means. Despite their pronounced hatred for the United States and its policies, these groups perceive it as a fertile environment for fundraising and recruitment. They know this country's open, innocent-until-proven-guilty nature, where criminals and victims have rights. The Constitution provides them protection from government prosecution. Loosely-affiliated groups of radical terrorists, like the one comprised of individuals who conspired in the bombing of the World Trade Center, remain a primary concern to the FBI. These groups are difficult to identify and do not easily conform to the rigid categorizations typically used by Western law enforcement organizations. Radical terrorist groups could avoid detection until they had committed a terrorist act. Membership is fluid, with the leadership or chain of command not readily identifiable. Until the World Trade Center bombing, international terrorist acts within the United States were rare and may remain so. That incident, however, shattered the illusion that the United States is immune from terrorism, and the reality was punctuated by the Oklahoma and Arizona events.

CHAPTER THREE

ISRAELI INTELLIGENCE AND DOMESTIC

COUNTERTERRORISM

Long before Israel petitioned for independence in 1948, it was evident to the British and the Arabs living in the area that a homeland was in the making for emigrating Jews. To the British, this meant yet another inconvenience in a land of uncertainty and instability, but to the Arabs living there, this was intolerable. Several terrorist incidents actually took place before Israel's statehood. On April 15, 1936, several armed Palestinians blocked a road and stopped about twenty vehicles to demand money for weapons and ammunition. One truck carrying crates of chickens to Tel Aviv had a Jewish driver and a Jewish passenger. A third Jew was in another car. For reasons known only to them, the Palestinians rounded up the three men and shot them, killing two and wounding the other. The following day, two members of a well-established, dissident Zionist militia group, *Irgun Bet*, drove to a farming shack east of Tel Aviv, knocked on the door, and fired inside, killing one Arab and badly wounding another. The British police and Arabs assumed that the attack was retaliatory "If the perpetrators had imagined that they would thus put an end to the bloodshed in Palestine, they were very soon to be disappointed."

As that week progressed, unrest and instability became the norm. Funerals turned into angry demonstrations, the Jewish Sabbath became a free-for-all for Jewish thugs to assault Arabs, and rumors became tacit permission to cause more violence. By the standards of earlier and later conflicts in the Middle East, this kind of violence and bloodshed was minor, but it was a warning of things to come. Arabs feared the expansionist nature of the Zionist enterprise, while Zionist land purchases continued in the wave of Jewish immigration that began after Hitler became Germany's chancellor. On 19 April, four days after the ambush by the Palestinians, life in the Tel

Aviv area returned to normal. Hundreds of Jews went to their offices and businesses in Jaffa. Then the trouble started with a rumor: three Syrian laborers and a local Arab woman had been killed in Tel Aviv. It was not true, but by nine o'clock that morning, large crowds of Arabs had gathered outside the government offices demanding the bodies of the "victims " Many Jews were stabbed or beaten up. However, many were given shelter in Arab homes. Still, others managed to get back to Tel Aviv via water transportation. In the ensuing melee, the British managed to quell the disturbance, but two Arabs and nine Jews were killed. A state of emergency was declared by the British authority.

The *Haganah* militia operated a semi-clandestine arm, a collection of volunteers conducting somewhat amateurish intelligence for the Histadrut labor federation. They were not in the right place before the Jaffa riots, or they neglected to see the signs. The Jews were shocked by the timing and strength of the Arab opposition. Unfortunately for those that died, the Haganah intelligence officers had seen no reason to report movements they had monitored around the main Jaffa mosque. Immediately after the riots, Arabs began attacking Jews everywhere, in cities and isolated areas. Arab stevedores went on strike, which crippled Jaffa's port. This went on for several months, but the Jews did not retaliate physically, choosing instead the diplomatic and political route. They tried to convince the British to crack down on the perpetrators. They also attempted to persuade the Palestine government that they were dealing with criminals and not a politically inspired rebellion. All of this was to no avail because the strike and the violence in Jaffa continued. Events had finally convinced the Haganah that security was now an overriding concern. The intelligence division recruited Jews who had extensive Arab contacts to gather information. They believed that human intelligence (HUMINT) was the best way to develop intelligence based on the activities of Arabs co-existing with Jews so that they would not continue to be caught unaware by dissident Palestinians. The Haganah policy was now "know the enemy."

The Jewish HUMINT sources were mainly merchants, farmers, and land developers. Because they had many Arab contacts in their day-to-day endeavors, they also had the opportunity to converse about Arab activities and perspectives. They were also able to recruit reliable Arab sources. These Arabs were not necessarily interested in money for these services but in revenge. Most of them had been persecuted by other Arabs because of ties of commerce and real estate sales to Jews, so they had strong personal reasons for wanting to neutralize or eliminate those persecutors. They expected the J vs. to offer them refuge when they were attacked or even defense of their homes. The Jews took advantage of this dependence and built reliable, complete dossiers on dissident Arabs n. At the same time, the Political Department of the *Haganah* tried various means to foment discord within the enemy camp through bribery and disinformation. By this time, eighty Jewish lives had been lost in the violence, and it was clear that intelligence work was becoming increasingly important.

By 1938, the Arabs engaged in a full-fledged revolt against the Zionists. The Jews were constantly haranguing the British to punish those rebels involved in the attack so that they would be deterred, but to no avail. The Arabs were very successful, capturing areas and regularly attacking police stations. An eccentric British officer, Charles Wingate, developed Special Night Squads (SNS) composed of a mixed force of British soldiers and *Haganah* volunteers to fight back. Eventually, they were as successful as the Arab rebels. The SNS accomplishments encouraged the *Haganah* to be bolder, use night ambushes, and go out and meet their Arab enemy on his own ground in a preemptive attack. Even after this British officer had been reassigned, the *Haganah* continued these activities and became quite efficient. By 1939, the Arab rebellion was waning. Their leader, Abdel-Rahim al-Haj Muhammad, was killed by the British army in a Samarian village, and rebel gangs had no stomach to fight anymore. They fled to Syria, and the Palestinians left behind were deeply divided without leadership. Although this was a tremendous military coup for the Zionists, diplomatically, it was disastrous. The British government decided against partitioning Palestine and severely restricted Jewish immigration and land sales to Jews. British authorities, intending to crack down, arrested Hagcmah members. They were particularly interested in the activities of Jewish fishermen involved in illegal immigration. The make-shift intelligence system of the Haganah had to be rearranged after these arrests. The national command set up a counter-espionage department that monitored Jews who collaborated with the British, and the right-wing dissidents of the Irgun Jewish communists were also under surveillance. By 1940, a joint country-wide intelligence service, Sherut Yediot or the Shai, was formed, and all of the various intelligence departments of the *Haganah* were placed under their auspices. The Shai was the first formal intelligence organization created by the Zionists.

By 1946, the Zionists knew a full-scale war with the Arabs was imminent. The Allies had liberated the Nazi death camps in Europe. It was under intense moral pressure to grant the Jews a homeland of their own Finally, the British, propelled by the United States, stopped trying to halt Jewish immigration into the area and turned it over to the United Nations. The United Nations General Assembly appointed a Special Commission on Palestine, which recommended that the British withdraw and the country be partitioned into separate Jewish and Arab states. These recommendations were endorsed by the General Assembly and accepted by the Jews, Palestinian

Arabs, and neighboring Arab states. However, they rejected the proposal outright. Hostilities perpetrated by Arabs against Jews were sporadic at first, and the Haganah did nothing because they believed this to be an initial wave of anger that would pass. When the violence continued and escalated, the *Haganah* became aggressively defensive, occasionally launching massive retaliatory strikes on Arab villages harboring armed rebels. The Arabs brought in "volunteers," including Iraqi, Syrian, and Jordanian soldiers. They reinforced the Palestinian irregulars and assisted in large-scale attacks against outlying Jewish settlements. The British were now concerned about withdrawing with as few casualties as possible, so their interference was minimal. The *Haganah* took advantage of the British lack of concern and went on the offensive, capturing the large Arab centers in Haifa, Tiberias, Jaffa, and parts of Jerusalem.

This triggered the most significant exodus of the Palestinian Arabs; by the time Israel was established, approximately three-hundred thousand Arabs had fled Palestine. When the war ended, approximately seven-hundred thousand refugees were in various Arab states. The Shai was ill-prepared for the war because its activities involved political rather than military intelligence. David Ben-Gurion, Israel's first prime minister, believed they lacked "direction and systematic thinking." Although they had made considerable improvements since their inception and exhibited increasing professionalism, the Shai remained a part-time, amateur intelligence service. They were unaware of the coming war with the Arabs, even though all events made this the inevitable conclusion. The *Shai's* human resources and energies were still committed to keeping tabs on Jewish Communists and right-wing dissidents such as the *Irgun* and the *Stem Gang*.

The *Shai's* failure to warn the *Haganah* of Syria's military deployments along the border and its mist ken anticipation of Arab rioting prompted Ben Gurion to set up an inquiry committee. They concluded that the Arab informants were losing their value and better, more well-placed informants were needed in Lebanon, Egypt, Syria, and Jordan. After the fact, when the Palestinians and the Israelis were well into the war, the *Shai* decided it was time to determine the nature and aims of enemy operations. They decided wiretapping would be the best method to gather intelligence and had an entire network set up. This method was imminently successful and more than made up for their past inadequacies. In fact, they upstaged military intelligence by accurately predicting the numbers, routes, and objectives of the Arab Legion and the Iraqis. In general, however, all the intelligence organizations had failed to gather practical intelligence for the Zionist cause. The *Haganah* operations branch felt they had a "fundamental intelligence blindness" and could not plan effectively. Ben-Gurion knew that their - intelligence apparatus had to be reformed, and there must be a clear separation between military and political intelligence. The *Shai* was dismantled, and its functions evolved into several new bodies under the *Sherut HaModi 'in* or the Intelligence Defense Service. By 1949, it consisted of eleven departments, and this structure was maintained for ten years. He also created an "internal *Shai,*" the General Security Service *(Shenit HaBitachon HaKali*) or Shin Bet. All of these came under the auspices of the Israeli Defense Force (IDF) Intelligence Service.

Until 1950, the *Shin Bet* (equivalent to the FBI in the United States) remained administratively within the framework of the IDF, which provided cover, services, military ranks, and pay. The head of the *Shin Bet* at that time, Isser Harel, felt that the new state of Israel needed a purely civilian security service because the military was providing minimal protection anyway. In early 1950, a compromise was reached, and the Shin Bet came under the Defense Ministry, and then later, it became autonomous, reporting directly to the prime minister. The *Shin Bet* was responsible for the routine physical security of classified information and government and defense establishment premises from the beginning. Their most important work, however, involved counter-espionage and domestic subversion, with particular attention devoted to Israel's Arab minority. Arab Communists and their links outside the country were an early priority. The *Shin Bet* accurately perceived the internal Arab danger and lobbied heavily for continued Israeli military rule in Arab areas for security reasons. The cease-fire line with the Jordanian West Bank was long, ill-defined, and ill-protected, and just beyond it lived hundreds of thousands of refugees. Whenever Arab spies were captured, they were portrayed in a sensationalist and demonic light. This was an attempt by the *Shin Bet* to make Israeli citizens aware of what was in their midst and, therefore, to offer help in the form of HUMINT. Many Jewish immigrants from Arab countries were constantly followed, and they reported that they had been offered money by Arabs to spy for hostile intelligence services, especially the Jordanians.

After Israel's stunning and unexpected victory in the Six-Day War, which began on June 5, 1967, they realized they were unprepared for its consequences. By June 10, with the West Bank, East Jerusalem, and the Gaza Strip under complete Israeli control, one of the first tasks they had to undertake was to work out how they would control a large and hostile Arab population. The *Shin Bet*, Mossad, and Aman (military intelligence) knew there would be terrorists in their midst. One intelligence operative defined the main security goal: "To isolate the terrorist from the general population and deny him shelter and assistance even though the natural sympathy of that population is with the terrorists and not the Israeli administration." This new intelligence threat required the three Israeli intelligence organizations to add new duties to their operations. *Aman* retained its overall responsibility for national intelligence and set collection and research priorities for the two other intelligence community components. The *Shin Bet* was given control of operational intelligence in the occupied territories, and *Mossad* was ordered to increase its targeting and penetration of Palestinian organizations abroad.

The *Shin Bet* was not prepared for the task it faced. Although their reserve workforce, particularly Arab speakers, had been mobilized, it was sometime before those new recruits were trained for operational deployment. "The service wasn't ready to take over such a large area and many people. Our only previous experience was in the Gaza Strip in 1956, and we assumed that the same would happen, that it would all be over and we'd be leaving in a few months," a senior *Shin Bet* officer revealed. The *Shin Bet* had developed into a highly professional security and counter-espionage organization whose two main tasks had been the control of the Arab minority and countering the threat of hostile foreign intelligence operations on Israeli soil. The closure of all Soviet Bloc embassies after the rupture of diplomatic relations in 1967 had freed some of the service's counterintelligence personnel for other duties. For the first few weeks after the end of hostilities, the Palestinians still existed in shock. By July, however, the *Shin Bet* had received indications that surprise had finally given way to anger, and there were signs of readiness to begin a civil disobedience campaign organized by the Palestinian Liberation Organization (PLO) against the occupation authorities. One factor contributing to their anger was the large number of Israelis who started to go out and see the sights their new territory had to offer and hunt for bargains in the East Jerusalem and Hebron souks.

Fatah, a Palestinian militant splinter group that had operated in Jordan and had not participated in the war, began to stir up rebellion. Their military wing announced:

> *"Our organization has decided to continue struggling against the Zionist conqueror. We plan to operate far from the Arab states so they will not suffer Israeli reprisals for fedayeen actions. It will therefore be impossible to hold the Arab people responsible for our war. Our organization is the organization of the Palestinian people, and we are*

united in our resolve to free our stolen homeland from the hands of the Zionists."

These words projected more confidence and preparation than the Palestinians possessed to conduct the guerrilla operations they envisioned. Approximately five-hundred volunteers went through three-week military and ideological training courses at *Fatah* camps in Syria after being screened by a "security committee" to ensure they were not Israeli agents. However, these crash courses were insufficient, and the Fatah security screen was also useless. When the first *fedayeen* entered the West Bank and Gaza Strip, they were often careless about concealing their tracks and identities. Having operated in Jordan and Egypt and dealing with the ruthless efficiency of their security services had made it difficult for the Palestinian national movement to build up infrastructure before the war. Early operations were amateurish, and the organizational cells were too large. Yasir Arafat, chairman of the PLO, and his deputies attributed these setbacks to: "the efficiency of the Israeli secret services and the carelessness of our fighters."

Arafat arrived in the West Bank and set up headquarters. He was impatient and pressed for immediate action when establishing bases and garnering gradual support would have been more prudent. As it was, he did little more than test the waters by conferring with supporters and raising morale. He eventually was forced to flee the area disguised as a woman after the Shin Bet had discovered his safe house. These victorious beginnings made the Shin Bel a powerful security force with whom the PLO had to deal. They had the advantage of putting their counterterrorist plans into action while Fatah was in the first stage of the organization before the onset of sabotage operations. Although the *Shin Bet's* successes were not well-known to Israelis due to military censors, the Palestinians were aware of their exploits and lived in fear. The other Israeli intelligence services began to respect the *Shin Bet's* professionalism, and close cooperation resulted, making *Fatah's* exploits less successful. One security officer said of *Shin Bet*, "The big change was that we were no longer just collecting intelligence. We went operational in our own right." From the outset, the *Shin Bet* proved adept at dealing with classic domestic terrorism. For example, a well-known Fatah cell operating in the Jerusalem area was arrested quickly after an explosion at the Fast Hotel in September 1967 and an abortive bomb attempt at the crowded Zion Square cinema in October 1967. No one was injured, but the cinema attack set a dangerous and worrying precedent; this was the first time Palestinians had tried to attack a purely civilian target. The head of this cell had recruited about thirty people, most of whom had been trained in Syria. Many were also members of Jerusalem's African community, descendants of Muslim pilgrims.

Two young African women were arrested immediately after the cinema bomb attempt, and in no time, the *Shin Bet* had a lead. The two women were amateurs. Under light interrogation, they gave everything away, providing the *Shin Bet* with the names of their comrades, their whereabouts, precise information about their training in Syria, their infiltration routes, and the organization of other cells in the West Bank. Within forty-eight hours, the entire cell had been rounded up, and the *Shin Bet* had uncovered arms, explosives, and vehicles. By the end of the first year of occupation, the West Bank was relatively quiet, but work was always to be done. The *Shin Bet* estimated that there were still between one-hundred and two-hundred Palestinian activists hiding in the collection of houses built around the narrow alleyways of the old Casbah in the Palestinian-dominated town of Nablus. They feared that if the core of the *fedayeen* was not broken up, they would be able to train and organize uninterrupted, improving their guerrilla tactics. The Israeli government, specifically Moshe Dayan, the defense minister, was reluctant to roust a community and disturb their peace unless the *Shin Bet* could guarantee they were sure of their suspects. Dayan gave the go-ahead when a Palestinian was assassinated for collaborating with the Israelis. The Shin Bet rounded up thousands of Palestinian men living in the Casbah and paraded them in front of masked informants. When all was said and done, the *Shin Bet* found two arms caches and arrested seventy-four people identified as guerrillas.

Although initially, *Fatah* had announced they would not be operating in Arab states, that philosophy changed as the *Shin Bet* became more adept at sniffing them out, and escape was imperative. Often, those terrorists that fled the *Shin Bet* raids would cross the river back into Jordan, which forced the Israelis to conduct reprisal raids on Jordanian army positions. This naturally increased the strain between King Hussein of Jordan and the Palestinians. The *Shin Bet* also used infiltration effectively. "A special effort was made to plant informers in terrorist bases in Jordan and to infiltrate them into networks operating inside Israeli-administered territories." one security expert wrote later. The Palestinians believed that penetration was extensive and worried about it constantly but did not have the power or expertise to stop it or put it to use. They tried to claim that they had many double agents operating for them, but Israeli sources insisted that these claims were false or at least vastly exaggerated. The *Shin Bet* insisted there were no known PLO penetrations of their operations. Exploiting Palestinian suspicions was also a successful technique used by the *Shin Bet.* They would "casually" mention a "collaborator" in front of a prisoner during an interrogation and then release or deport him. In many cases, the freed Palestinian would denounce his colleagues as traitors, fueling the already intense fear of Israeli penetration and creating internal purges via "remote control."

PLO factions were incredibly naive during the early days of their terrorist operations. During the training process, they obviously did not instill loyalty in their volunteers, which made the Shin Bet'sjob much easier. One captured terrorist could do immense damage to a cell. The *Shin Bet* would take a captive, dress him up in an IDF uniform and dark glasses and take a tour of the West Bank. As they traversed the area from north to south, the terrorist would point out people he had trained with. Massive arrests would follow, which, in turn, would increase Palestinian suspicions of Israeli penetration. An unwitting ally of the *Shin Bet* was Jordan. The PLO claimed that Israeli penetration was responsible for the confrontations between the Palestinians and the Jordanian army, but their arrogance infuriated King Hussein. He could not accept creating an independent Palestinian state within his kingdom. When the Popular Front for the Liberation of Palestine (PFLP) hijacked three international airliners and set them down in a desert airfield in Jordan, the *Shin Bet* informed them that their relatives (measuring in the hundreds) were being held hostage pending the outcome of this terrorist act. The passengers were released unharmed, and the aircraft was blown up.

King Hussein responded to these actions by turning his army on the Palestinians, thousands of whom were annihilated. This became known among the Palestinians as Black September. Scores of *fedayeen* fled from the East Bank after another confrontation with the Jordanian army, and seventy-two surrendered to the Israelis rather than face a bloody conflict. The Israelis used those who were extremely grateful to still be alive to contact and identify other groups, who were then rounded up by the *Shin Bet*. In the Gaza Strip, which was much more densely populated with Palestinians, the *Shin Bet* had more difficulty isolating PLO and PFLP terrorists. In this area, the terrorists were more firmly entrenched, and the appalling physical conditions under which the refugees had to live made them more sympathetic to the rebel cause. Eventually, the *Shin Bet* had to work closely with the Israeli army. An elite commando unit was ordered to comb the area until every terrorist was found. In the refugee camps, adult males were randomly stopped and searched; curfews were imposed on the bases; and the army was supplied regularly with a list of wanted terrorists. Before the army assisted the *Shin Bet*, there were thirty-four terrorist incidents recorded by July 1971. By December of that same year, only one terrorist incident had occurred. The *Shin Bet-Army* cooperation was highly effective. The massacre of eleven Israeli athletes in Munich was a blot on the Shin Bet record and a severe blow to the image they had built up with their successes in Israel. The security of the athletes was their responsibility, while any intelligence information on Palestinian terrorist activities was the responsibility of the *Mossad.* According to the *Mossad* chief, his organization had received intelligence about a PLO unit flying in from the Middle East to somewhere in Europe and had passed it to the Shin Bet, arguing that the report was vague almost to the point of uselessness. An inquiry into the security lapse led three senior Shin Bet executives to be dismissed. Golda Meir, the prime minister, felt this would help restore confidence in the security service. The relative success of the *Shin Bet* after the Six-Day War prevented the Palestinians from launching a people's war when their ideology required it. The occupied territories never became Algeria or Vietnam, as envisioned by the PLO. The Israelis constructed a security system based on the "carrot and stick" method, a fruitful gambit. Although the *Shin Bet* was successful, this forced the Palestinian terrorists to operate abroad, which was much more difficult for *Mossad* to handle without the backing of the Israeli army.

ISRAELI COUNTERTERRORISM (1980 - 1989)

Although the *Shin Bet* was acknowledged internationally as the premier domestic security service, it was certainly not without its share of scandal and corruption. They had developed their craft over more than a decade and had become very adept at flushing out terrorists and preventing most terrorist activities within Israel and the occupied territories. It might be said that the scandals erupted at this time because the intelligence services of Israel were attempting to stay on top of their game in a changing world. Palestinian terrorists were beginning to catch up with Israeli intelligence methods, and it was becoming more difficult for those agencies to stay on top of the Palestinians. The first *Shin Bet* scandal began on April 12, 1984. Four teenage Palestinians from the Gaza Strip boarded the number 300 bus in Tel Aviv en route to the southern town of Ashkelon. About halfway through the journey, one of the thirty-five passengers, who had somehow become suspicious of the four Arabs and their intentions and had tried in vain to warn the driver of his fears, jumped off the bus shouting: "Terrorists, terrorists!" One of the Palestinians threatened the bus driver with a knife and a hand grenade. A second hijacker brandished some spray can. The third took up a position in the center of the bus, holding a briefcase from which wires were protruding, and the fourth said he had a grenade. They informed the passengers that they had no quarrel with them and allowed a pregnant woman passenger to disembark. She alerted the police, and roadblocks were set up, but the bus continued. A few miles south of Gaza City, soldiers shot out the bus's rear tires, bringing it to a standstill. The driver escaped and was beaten by soldiers who mistook him for one of the hijackers.

When the defense minister was informed, an elite army unit was in position around the bus awaiting orders. The head of the *Shin Bet*, Avraham Shalom, his deputy, and five other *Shin Bet* field operatives and executives were also present. Negotiations began with the first hijacker, who was still standing by the driver's seat. He demanded to see the Egyptian ambassador and the immediate release of five-hundred Palestinian prisoners. Several journalists and photographers had appeared by then to record the event. At dawn the next day, soldiers stormed the bus. The first and second hijackers were killed, and most passengers had thrown themselves to the floor.

The other two hijackers were overpowered and badly beaten to stun them. When they were brought off the bus, Brigadier General Yitzhak Mordechai, commander of the elite unit, questioned them. By his own admission, he pistol-whipped them to get answers to his various questions. Although the hijackers were dazed, they were alive when handed over to the *Shin Bet*. As they were led away to a nearby wheat field, photographers recorded the .-vent on film. Israel Radio reported that two terrorists had been killed in the assault and two others captured. Later that day, however, in response to repeated questioning by journalists, an IDF spokesman said that two terrorists had been killed in the storming of the bus and that the two others had died on their way to the hospital in Ashkelon. Doubts began to emerge about the truth of the official statements. The Jerusalem correspondent for the New York Times ignored the military censor restrictions and reported suspicions that the two living hijackers had been killed after their capture. Other media and the IDF were also very confused. The defense ministry ordered an inquiry into the affair.

Against better judgment, the defense ministry allowed the *Shin Bet* to appoint their own man to represent the security service on the board of inquiry. The *Shin Bet* insisted that this would prevent friction between them and the army. Later on. However, it was apparent that the *Shin Bet* member on the board of inquiry was passing details of the investigation back to Avraham Shalom, the director of *Shin Bet*. With this information, the *Shin Bet* was able to work out a cover-up. After the autopsy was completed, the board published its report. They found that both terrorists had died of fractured skulls and that unspecified "security forces" members had committed crimes. The *Shin Bet* witnesses described to the investigators how they saw General Mordechai standing before a kneeling terrorist and kicking him in the head. Others said that he had used his pistol like "a hammer." The *Shin Bet* had agreed to set up Mordechai as the prime suspect. The witnesses were briefed by GSS legal advisers before appearing in front of the inquiry and were ordered to report back to headquarters afterward to describe what had happened. It was a very professional cover-up. Mordechai realized he was being framed and, because of his popularity, was able to find witnesses who contradicted those of the Shin Bet. Nine soldiers described how *Shin Bet* agents had sealed off the wheat field while dealing with the hijackers. They reported what happened as an "organized lynch " Unfortunately, this did not help because, although there was insufficient evidence to charge Mordechai with the killings, it was recommended that he, five *Shin Bet* men, and three policemen be tried for assault. A special disciplinary court acquitted all.

The deputy of the *Shin Bet* demanded the resignation of Shalom. He approached Shimon Peres, the prime minister, and offered to tender his resignation if that was what it took to obtain Shalom's removal. Peres refused, and the deputy took the demand outside the service to the attorney-general, Yitzhak Zamir. The attorney-general and his aides cross-examined the deputy for days and were finally convinced of the truth Israel Television reported on May 1986 that Professor Zamir intended to prosecute a "very senior official in a compassionate state service. "That person was named the next day as Avraham

Shalom, and it became public knowledge in Israel that the head of *Shin Bet* was accused of withholding information about the killings, putting pressure on witnesses, and tampering with evidence. Shalom knew ultimately that he had to go, and he resigned on June 26 after it was announced that he and three other officials had been granted pardons by President Chaim Herzog. Later, when a new attorney-general was installed, the police forwarded their findings of the case, including the statements of thirty-nine witnesses. This report clarified that the two hijackers were killed on Shalom's orders. Shalom claimed he gave orders based on a conversation with Shamir in November 1983, in which the treatment of captured terrorists was discussed. Shamir informed the police that he remembered the meeting but "looking back, I must say that could not be understood as permission to take prisoners, question them and then kill them." The Justice Ministry team concluded that Shamir had not known of the order to kill the terrorists or of the subsequent cover-up.

The attorney general decided the case was closed because Shalom and the other players had already been pardoned. Other scandals followed, but the *Shin*

Bet was able to weather them. By the end of the decade, their high-profile approach and considerable successes in dealing with the *intifada* endeared them again to the Israelis. The unrest changed as the West Bank and Gaza Strip Palestinians tired of their long struggle and the human and economic sacrifices required. The mass stone-throwing demonstrations gave way to hit-and-run attacks by small groups of activists. This kind of activity was on what the *Shin Beth* had cut its teeth. The Palestinian activists were organized in classic cell-like structures with which the *Shin Bet* was familiar. Operating closely with the army, *Shin Bet* agents tracked down and killed or captured the members of two small *Fatah*-affiliated armed groups. They had also arrested hundreds of members of the military wing of the *Hamas* movement in the Gaza Strip. Some Palestinians argued that this was no great coup because *Hamas* members were not used to operating clandestinely and therefore were an easy target.

ISRAELI COUNTERTERRORISM (1990s)

Early in this decade, the *Shin Bet* showed it could hold its own with its long-tried modus operandi. It also helped that the *intifada* was having bad luck, suffering blow after blow to its cause. In May 1990, after an abortive seaborne attack by the Palestine Liberation Front on the Israeli coast, the United States halted its dialogue with the PLO, robbing the organization of its greatest political achievement. This coincided with the collapse of the Labor-Likud national unity coalition and its replacement with a new right-wing Likud government. This was another blow to the legitimacy of the Palestinian's cause, as Likud was well-known for its stand against Palestinian autonomy. When Iraq invaded Kuwait in August, Palestinians enthusiastically supported Saddam Hussein. Being on the side of the defeated caused them political and economic damage, hurt their dialogue with the Israeli left (their only hope in Israel), and halted vital financial support from Arab countries who had stood against Iraq's invasion. All this made life easier for the *Shin Bet*. They were spurred by the conviction that internal security had to be maintained so that Israel could negotiate from a strong position on the future of the West Bank and Gaza Strip.

THE ASSASSINATION OF YITZHAK RABIN

Although the *Shin Bet* began its counterterrorism operation with Jewish right-wing groups, the rise of the Palestinian terrorists took precedence. Right-wing groups were watched but largely ignored. Since the Six-Day War, violent, hate-filled Jewish groups have been in the political landscape. Their platform is based on the fact that the Sinai, West Bank, Gaza Strip, and Golan Heights must be retained as part of Israel's biblical birthright by violence if necessary. Any Jew who opposes them is a traitor to the cause. Although many right-wing groups have existed since the founding of the Israeli state (Irgim, Stem Gang), the most violent has been Kach (Thus), founded by American-born Meir Kahane (who also founded the Jewish Defense League). Kahane's rhetoric was so flammable in 1983 a lone right-winger threw a grenade into a crowd of Peace Now ralliers, killing one Israeli man. He based this action on encouragement from Kahane's speeches. It was the first time in a long time that a Jew had used violence against fellow Jews for political reasons. Although Kach has diminished in influence, it still creates trouble. The group often makes telephone threats against journalists and politicians and takes responsibility for any violent act against Arabs. Only after Kach devotee Baruch Goldstein sprayed a Hebron mosque with automatic-rifle fire in 1994, killing twenty-nine worshipers, did the *Shin Bet* begin to concentrate more fully on violent right-wing groups.

On November 4, 1995, during a peace rally, Yitzhak Rabin, the prime minister of Israel, was assassinated by Yigal Amir, a law student. Amir and his conspirators have been linked to Eyal, a Kach offshoot. This group is based at Tel Aviv's Bar Ilan University. Although its activities have usually tended toward threats and harassment rather than outright violence, they tend to believe that any act, including murder, is justified if it thwarts the peace process. Immediately after the assassination, the *Shin Bet* began thoroughly investigating events connected to the operation in all its stages. After the data were gathered, the Director established an internal investigation committee to expand the investigation and the inquiry into the circumstances. The members of this committee were three former *Shin Bet* division heads who had retired at least ten years ago: Uzi Berger, former head of the *Shin Bet* Operations Division. Savinoam Avivi, previously head of the Shm Bet Protection Division, and Kafi Malka, who served as heads of the *Shin Bet* Operations Division, Administration Division, and Protection Division in Europe.

The Internal Committee was asked in its letter of appointment to examine the following issues and the responsibility of the chain of command for these issues:

1. 1 The preparations for the operation.
2. The intelligence for the event.
3. The coordination of the intelligence with security inputs.
4. Coordination with the various elements that provided security for the event: police, police anti-terror unit, hospital, and others.
5. Performance of the unit during the event while emphasizing its performance during the assassination and the Prime Minister's evacuation.

The committee was given full access to all the material requested and allowed to interview those persons it thought relevant to the event. They worked continuously from November 5 to November 8 and submitted these conclusions to the Director of the *Shin Bet*:

1. 1 Planning failure: the committee points to a failure in planning in that a critical segment of the security operation for the event — and the professionalism appropriate for its security — was not considered.

2. Operational failure: the planning failure led to an operational failure in the security of this same critical segment. During the event, the planning failure was discerned, and several directives were given to correct the deficiencies in the critical segment. The directives were partial and were issued late. Their implementation as well was not complete.

3. 3 Due to the planning and security deficiencies and the failure to correct the holes, the murderer succeeded in approaching the Prime Minister within a lethal distance.

4. The committee found that the bodyguard, who jumped on the murderer and did not fire at him, had exercised correct judgment, given the circumstances, a comparative run-through of firing a bullet, and field conditions. The committee commended the performance of the bodyguard, who was wounded during the event.

5. The committee was not asked to examine — and therefore did not relate to — the performance of the police and did not deal with issues related to the prevention of incitement, et cetera, as being relevant to the event.

6. The committee pointed to the direct responsibility of three persons: the head of the Government Unit for VIP Protection, the head of the Operations Branch, and the commander for the event. The committee recommended that the Director of the Shin Bet draw the necessary conclusions regarding those responsible for the failure and its occurrence.

7. The committee found that the head of the Protection Division bears the responsibility for the system's poor functioning. The protection plan was presented to him during his visit to the

event, and during the event itself, he pinpointed many deficiencies and ordered that they be corrected. The defects were corrected late and incompletely.

The Director of the *Shin Bet* decided to recommend to Acting Prime Minister Shimon Peres that the head of the Protection Division, the head of the Government VIP Protection Unit, the head of the unit's Operations Branch, and the commander of the event be suspended until all the examinations related to the tragic incident are completed, including a state commission of inquiry should it be decided to establish one Acting Prime Minister Peres approved the Director's decisions Later, the Director met with those heads of the divisions mention previously and told them of the committee's report and its conclusions and about his decision to suspend them immediately until all the investigations are completed. The head of the Protection Division then asked to resign from the *Shin Bet*, and his resignation was accepted. Other *Shin Bet* officials were appointed to fill in for those who were suspended or left, and appropriate measures were taken to ensure the Shin Bet's operational capability while implementing the lessons learned. The Director of the *Shin Bet* then convened the entire organization and presented the committee's conclusions and the decisions he had made in their wake. He discussed the future of the Shin Bet. He noted the immediate successful deployment of the largest protection operation ever in Israel, which had occurred over the previous forty-eight hours. The Director emphasized the *Shin Bet's* obligation to defend the State of Israel and its leaders and ministers against Arab and Jewish terrorism, which continues to threaten Israel.

On November 21, 1995, it was announced that Amir had once worked as a security guard abroad and had been trained by the *Shin Bet.* An accomplice, Avaishi Raviv, was an informer (and an alleged agent provocateur) secretly reporting to the Shin Bet while reportedly handing out fliers of Rabin dressed as a Nazi SS officer. An intelligence expert, Yossi Melman, stated, "There was a colossal failure of the General Security Service which led to Rabin's assassination. They had many tips and leads about Amir's intention to murder the prime minister, and they ignored them." This information has shifted the focus of blame away from right-wing extremists to the failures of the Shin

Bet" Although recent events have thrown the *Shin Bet* into an unfavorable light, history has shown that they have been supremely effective in fighting domestic terrorism. In the future, they will have more on which to concentrate, and it will be necessary to distrust Jews and Arabs. In today's world climate, anyone can be a terrorist in Israel, and the Shin Bet is up to the challenge.

CHAPTER FOUR

BRITISH COUNTERTERRORISM AND NORTHERN IRELAND

The previous chapters on the FBI and the Shin Bet have discussed those organizations' methods, successes, and scandals in their continuing fight against domestic terrorism. In Great Britain, however, domestic terrorism has been fought on all fronts by different organizations. When the "Great Trouble" began in 1969, Northern Ireland tried to control the violence perpetrated by the Irish Republican Army (IRA) with the Royal Ulster Constabulary (RUC), a country police force. Unfortunately for them, they were understaffed and unprepared to engage the IRA. The leader of Northern Ireland petitioned the British Parliament for assistance, which came in the form of the British army. This chapter will examine the various means British and Northern Ireland Loyalists employ to combat IRA terrorist acts. This will include a look at England's role through the use of MI5, MI6, the Army, and the Special Air Services, the effectiveness of the Royal Ulster Constabulary and other law enforcement groups within Ireland; the use of supergrasses; and the use of extralegal means to convict and incarcerate suspected terrorists Like Israel, the British have approached the IRA's terrorism campaign with thoroughness and precision.

BRITISH CONTRIBUTIONS TO COUNTERTERRORISM IN NORTHERN IRELAND

The Special Air Services (SAS) was first called to service in Northern Ireland when the breakdown in law and order occurred in August 1969. For a year, the violence between civil rights demonstrators and the RUC (backed by the "B" Specials, a reserve volunteer patrol group) had convinced the Protestants that civil war was imminent. The Catholic community and the Dublin government thought a pogrom was about to occur. The British and Protestant governments could not agree to what extent military support should reinforce law enforcement organizations. Finally, the British agreed to send support only if there was a complete breakdown of law and order and only after the Protestants' law enforcement organizations failed to control the situation. Unfortunately, this is what happened. In 1920, the British government planned to partition Ireland into the six counties of the North with its own Parliament in Belfast and another Parliament in Dublin to represent the twenty-six counties in the

Irish Free State. During this planning stage, when elections to the new parliaments were being organized, the British government was persuaded to protect unionists in the North from the IRA. IRA attacks became so numerous that the British authorized the Under-Secretary in Belfast to form the Special Constabulary (or "Specials") in October 1920.

The Specials were divided into three classes: Class "A" were full-time reserve police who were armed, equipped, uniformed, and paid the same wages as regular police. The "B" Specials were unpaid, except for a clothing allowance, and expected to carry out duties in their own areas on one or two nights per week. "C" Specials were simply men listed as available for emergency services and provided their own weapons. The "A" Specials eventually merged with the RUC and the "C" Specials were abolished, leaving only the "Bs." From the date of their establishment to the mid-1960s, the "B" Specials were very successful in countering IRA terrorist activities. While the RUC had a maximum strength of about thirty-five hundred, the "B" Specials could call up about twelve thousand volunteers to patrol, preventing the IRA from moving freely. An IRA historian, Pat Coogan, noted that the

Specials "were the rock on which any mass movement by the IRA in the North has inevitably foundered." In the increasing street rioting and violence of 1969, the Specials were not given special training in riot control or modern equipment such as riot shields. Also, the Loyalists were lobbying for support from the Labor government in London, so the Specials were eventually phased out. From July 1969, the Specials were only used minimally at the discretion of the RUC County Inspectors. They were reinstated fully on August 14 when the RUC almost lost control of a riot, and the government ordered the mobilization of the Specials. The number of mobilized men intimidated the smaller violent mobs.

On August 15, Northern Ireland's government asked the Labor government in London for assistance from the British army. By the 16th, the army had taken control of all riot areas without the aid of the RUC and the Specials. Northern Ireland's Prime Minister Chichester-Clarke and Harold Wilson, England's Prime Minister, met on August 19th to discuss the future security of Ireland. Although the record of the meeting remains secret, Wilson has stated in a television interview that a decision was made to dismiss the Specials. The disbanding of the "B" Specials significantly reduced the amount of street intelligence flowing to the government, which, in turn, was not helpful to the British soldiers. The intelligence available to the army was limited and tended to be inaccurate. By 1971, the hard-line Provisional IRA (PIRA) emerged with a bombing campaign. Averaging two explosions daily, the authorities became desperate to penetrate the terrorist network. The Ajmy adopted the "counter-gang" tactics developed during Kenya's Mau Mau period. These tactics, based on three separate factors, were designed to make a shift allegiance from one group to another and become an efficient, unrecognizable intelligence gatherer. The first factor (the carrot) introduces an incentive strong enough to make the man want to shift his loyalty. Then he must understand that failure will result in unpleasant consequences (the stick). Thirdly, he must be allowed to prove to himself and his friends that his action is not dishonorable.

ERA activists who were arrested were given the choice of imprisonment or undercover work for the British Army. They usually opted for the latter and were formed into the Special Detachment of the

Military Reconnaissance Force (MRF). The task of these MRFs was to drive around Belfast's Republican districts to identify their comrades in the IRA, who were then placed under surveillance or arrest. Unfortunately, not many MRF members lived to enjoy the promised freedom. Some attempted to become double agents, while others made the mistake of returning to their homes. They were eventually discovered by the IRA and shot or tortured during interrogations. This type of intelligence work did not satisfy the Protestant Government. In August 1971, against military advice, the Northern Ireland prime minister persuaded London to introduce internment without trial. This move alienated many uncommitted Catholics and exposed the lack of information collected by the security forces' intelligence system. Many of those people rounded up had had nothing to do with the IRA for years, while the real culprits remained on the loose. The result was a severe escalation of violence. While only fifty-nine people had been killed in two years from August 1969 to August 1971, an additional two-hundred thirty-one were killed in the following six months. The British government told the Northern Ireland prime minister that they were no longer willing to have their army directed by his government, and the responsibility for that part of security was transferred to London.

At about this time, the SAS were posted as individuals to Military Intelligence in Ulster. The Intelligence Director was a senior Secret Intelligence Service (MI6) officer traditionally concerned with intelligence collection outside the United Kingdom. This caused intense resentment in MI5, which was responsible for Ulster and domestic counterterrorism. The MI6 Intelligence Director had a direct line to the prime minister in London. There was also an intelligence officer from MI5 working in Northern Ireland who had a direct line to the Prime Minister. A third source of intelligence was the Army, which had developed fruitful relationships between their undercover agents and informers. Since both were at risk of discovery, these sources of information had to be kept close-hold. This resulted in turmoil for those in the field because they did not know to whom they had to report. Some intelligence officers believed the IRA's assassination often informers was due to a leak overlooked in the confusion. In 1974, more SAS officers were sent to control agents in the field to impose order on this chaos. There was political opposition from the Northern Ireland and London governments because both were involved in secret negotiations with the IRA. However, discovering a "doomsday" plan in a raid on IRA headquarters proved that the IRA was not serious about peace but playing for time.

The conflict in Ireland created some problems because, politically, London and Northern Ireland refused to see this as a war. In contrast, the soldiers and SAS operatives could not see it as anything else. A soldier reacting to what he thought was a wartime situation would suddenly find himself arrested and facing civil charges, which tended to be demoralizing. At this point, both governments were at a loss as to how to conclude this situation. They chose political solutions since direct confrontation was not as successful as they wanted.

THE PREVENTION OF TERRORISM ACT

The Prevention of Terrorism Act was legislated in 1974 in response to the campaign of violence the IRA sustained in Britain beginning in 1972. This intense violence was sustained for two years, and the citizens were terrified. The House Secretary, Mr. Roy Jenkins, introduced the Prevention of Terrorism (Temporary Provisions) Bill to Parliament, which passed in forty-two hours without amendment. The Act expired in May 1975, but an extension was successfully implemented. In 1976, a new Act was passed, adding a few more crimes, and again, it had to be renewed. By this time, the renewal process had become a formality. In 1984, another review by Earl Jellicoe resulted in the Prevention of Terrorism (Temporary Provisions) Act 1984. With this measure, international terrorism was added. 1989 the Act was greatly expanded and no longer limited to five years. The most important powers in preventing terrorism legislation in Great Britain relate to proscription, exclusion, and detention. There are three groups of crimes relevant to prescription. Belonging to the IRA or the Irish National Liberation Army is an offense in Britain, punishable by up to ten years in prison. Soliciting or inviting support for the IRA or INLA is also prohibited. Secondly, it is a crime to arrange, manage, or address any meeting of three or more persons if it is known that the meeting is to support or further the activities of these groups. Thirdly, any person who in a public place either wears any item of dress or wears, carries, or displays an article "in such a way or in such circumstances as to arouse reasonable apprehension that he is a member or supporter of a proscribed organization" may incur a severe penalty of a fine or up to six months in prison.

The exclusion powers of the Terrorism Act are the most widely disliked and controversial part of this legislation. The Secretary of State is satisfied that if any person has been involved in any part of acts of terrorism connected with Norther Ireland or is attempting to enter Great Britain to commit acts of terrorism, they may make an exclusion order against the suspected perpetrator A British citizen who has resided in England for at least three years is exempt so, in practice this law is aimed at the Irish in Britain. Exclusions are based on intelligence, forensic evidence, and/or previous convictions. Suppose a person is detained based on suspicion and remains silent during interrogation. This fact may be used against them because it shows training in "anti-interrogation" techniques, and they may be excluded. This violates the privilege against self-incrimination, which was anticipated with the formal destruction of the right to silence in Northern Ireland. The Prevention of Terrorism Act also includes the discretion to arrest without a warrant when a constable has reasonable grounds for suspecting an offense against the proscription, exclusion, or financial provisions. The power lies in the period of detention without charge that can follow from the arrest. The basic rule is that a suspect may be held for no more than forty-eight hours but in reality, this is not the case. A review officer, who must not have been directly involved in the case, studies the suspect's case "as soon as practicable after the beginning of the detention." The review officer can then continue to look at the case at twelve-hour intervals, but the incarceration can be prolonged if the review officer is not readily available.

The review officer can also authorize continued detention if two conditions exist. First, the officer must be satisfied that detention is necessary to preserve evidence relating to the offenses. Second, the officer must be confident that the investigation is being conducted thoroughly and quickly. The two-day detention can be further extended up to five days by order of the Secretary of State. When an application for such an extension is made, the review procedure described at length in the Act does not apply. It is futile to object and request a judicial review because, given the subject matter of the power involved, no court in England will dare to review a Home Secretary's decision. There are also no special guarantees in the Act about sleep, diet, or treatment of detainees, despite the greater length of time involved. Some government officials have discovered that detention may not necessarily occur for prosecution purposes. Sometimes a detainee is questioned about their political views, friends, and colleagues to gather background information that may be useful later. The police and the army have been known to arrest not only a person against whom there is firm evidence but also people connected with this person. This can defeat the whole purpose of detention by alienating the innocent and making them more sympathetic to the causes of the terrorists. Prescription, exclusion, and imprisonment have been fought by many British and Irish citizens who see these as infringing their civil rights. Although it is not explicitly mentioned in the Prevention of Terrorism Act, many of these allowances target Irish citizens. There is no bill of rights in Great Britain, but it has been frequently proposed as a solution to the perceived threat to political freedom. Its supporters have stipulated that it must list protected political liberties, such as freedom of expression, conscience, and religion. Parliament would not be permitted to pass laws that violate the terms of the Bill of Rights, and existing legislation would be capable of a challenge if it went against guaranteed freedoms.

THE USE OF SUPERGRASSES

The practice of using informants by Great Britain's police and prosecution authorities goes back several centuries. Informants have also been used in trials in Northern Ireland for the past fifteen years. In November 1981, the RUC arrested William Black in a Catholic area of North Belfast. A trial began in Belfast's Crown Court just over a year later. Thirty-eight people were accused of one-hundred eighty-four separate charges stemming from forty-five alleged incidents of violence. Black had agreed to cooperate with the authorities during his interrogation, providing the majority and, at times, the only evidence against the accused. Authorities like to call those who give this evidence "converted terrorists."

Still, scholars have pointed out that this term is erroneous because these individuals do not convert due to genuine repentance. Most of them cooperate in exchange for shorter prison sentences and immunity. A more popular and frequently used term is "supergrass." The development of supergrasses as the principal method of securing convictions in Ireland came from the Italian government's response to their political violence. In 1978 following the kidnapping and assassination of Aldo Moro, the Italian government introduced a new measure that provided for a substantial reduction in punishment if the accomplices detached themselves from the others and endeavored to secure the release of a victim. Subsequent legislation extended the notion of dissociation further by adding cooperation with the police to prevent criminal activity and/or to gather crucial evidence leading to the arrest of the conspirators. The Italian authorities expected true repentance from the terrorists, which went a long way in persuading the informers to participate fully. Authorities in Northern Ireland believed the Italians had found an excellent deterrent, but they were more pragmatic about human nature and the nature of terrorists. They were not interested in the motivation or beliefs of the supergrass. The fact that they turn is sufficient. Moreover, a repentant terrorist cannot be exploited in Ireland as in Italy.

Most supergrasses have been recruited during interrogation after arrest, although some have been drawn from those already imprisoned. The types of people who have been recruited have made the whole strategy questionable. One supergrass was described as a dangerous and ruthless terrorist, while another had an extensive criminal record. The inducements used by the authorities include money or a new life, but the most attractive was the offer of immunity from prosecution for the crimes they have committed. Although it is granted liberally in Northern Ireland, the prosecution and the public have expressed concern over the immunity of supergrasses involved in serious crimes. One supergrass who informed and was subsequently granted immunity later recanted and admitted to being an accomplice in the killing of an informer. The authorities then decided that immunity would be granted only to accomplices rather than the actual murders. Another objection to the use of supergrasses was the unreliability of witness testimony. At times, the supergrass is expected to provide information about many people covering hundreds of separate incidents stretching back many years. As experimental psychologists have proved, people forget information and incidents as the interval increases between the time of the information's acquisition and retrieval. It has also been found that it is possible for a subject to take the information provided to them, eventually believes it to be true, and replace their own correct version with that information. Supergrasses may unknowingly perjure themselves, thinking this specious testimony to be true.

From various accounts, the authorities were fully aware of the problems of inadequate recall and the pressure to produce results. Various supergrasses have stated the way police intervened in drawing up their statements. Others have described that the police have given them names, expecting them to implicate those people in terrorist activities. There are a lot of issues that must be considered during a supergrass trial. In ordinary criminal trials, where it is discovered that the witness has a criminal record, the jury is warned to treat that evidence with caution. However, in a supergrass trial, the case will rest almost exclusively on the evidence of a person who would be regarded with suspicion in other circumstances. A supergrass may recant, disappear or die before the case is trialed. In the case of retraction, the alleged terrorists are released unless another supergrass can be found to give evidence to hold them. The supergrass strategy has radically extended the role of criminal law uniquely. In a typical criminal trial, a witness testifies in an individual capacity with the understanding that their testimony will not have any wider consequences. The activities of a supergrass, however, will eventually affect family and friends, who may be used as pawns in the strategy. The police need the family and friends to support and maintain the supergrass in his commitment to be the principal witness. The IRA use the families and friends as hostages to make the supergrass recant. The use of supergrass evidence ultimately creates a climate of fear and distrust among those who engage in political violence and within the communities whose interests the strategy is supposed to serve. All the strategies tried in Northern Ireland have shown that the problem of political violence cannot be dealt with through conventional or radically modified criminal justice systems. While it may be possible to achieve "an acceptable level of violence," ultimately, the law has not successfully solved this particular problem.

CEASE FIRE?

England and the Republic of Ireland have a Joint Declaration of Peace. This was made on December 15, 1993, to "remove the conflict, to overcome the legacy of history and to heal the resulting divisions." The IRA followed almost one year later with a cease-fire declaration on August 31,1994. It included their belief that an opportunity for peace had been created by the Joint Declaration, and they were going to take advantage of it. The Combined Loyalist Military Command (CLMC), the military arm of the Loyalists, released their cease-fire statement on October 13, 1994, with the hope that everyone could "resolve to respect our differing views of freedom, culture, and aspiration and never again permit our political circumstances to degenerate into bloody warfare." Since the recent troubles began in Ireland in 1969, this latest attempt at peace seems to be the best weapon against domestic terrorism in Great Britain. Both the Loyalists and the Nationalists perpetrated terrorist activities, but it was usually retaliatory in nature with no real objective but revenge. In all those years, the political situation did not change, nor did the views of the Loyalists and the Nationalists Terrorism created a stalemate.

Both the Sinn Fein and the Progressive Unionist Party, the political arms of the warring factions, have seen the futility of the terrorism carried out by their military sections and now see England's offer of peace as an opportunity to negotiate and legitimize themselves worldwide. Although it has not been said, it seems more than a coincidence that they approached this solution after the PLO and Israel signed their peace agreement. Perhaps both sides see the futility of violence and are finally aware of how it has affected the populace and the economy. Their countries have been ravaged, poverty in the Republic of Ireland and Northern Ireland is at an all-time high, and families have been cruelly separated. The Irish are weary and seem ready for a peaceful change.

CHAPTER FIVE

COUNTERTERRORISM AND THE CONSTITUTION

The previous three chapters discussed the fight against domestic terrorism in three countries: the United States, Israel, and Great Britain. Each country has had a different domestic terrorist problem, and each has chosen to fight it differently based on cultural and constitutional constraints (or lack thereof). In the United States, domestic terrorism has never really been a problem in the past compared to Israel and Great Britain. In the 1960s, the FBI was concerned about reactions to civil rights and the negative response to the war in Viet Nam. Organizations such as the Ku Klux Klan and the Black Panthers were well-armed and not averse to using extreme violence and intimidation to further their goals. The FBI felt justified in violating the constitutional rights of the alleged terrorists to fight what they saw as a threat to the security of the United States. They were very successful, if not brutal.

While Great Britain and Israel seem to have settled their differences with the IRA and the Palestinians (at least for now), domestic terrorism has occurred in the United States after a long absence. As mentioned, the World Trade Center and the Oklahoma bombings have brought it to the forefront in the most tragic way. According to one source, there were signs that violence directed at the federal government was scheduled for April 19, 1995. Strategic links between militia groups and white supremacist organizations had been detected as early as October 1994 through various communique, racist publications, and law enforcement bulletins. A Klanwatch intelligence report pointed out the significance of the April 19 date among militia extremists. For more than a year, the Waco burning, the execution of Richard Wayne Snell (a white supremacist convicted of two murders in Arkansas), and the Ruby Ridge incident were the rallying cry of militia organizations against the federal government. They made these "injustices" known through meetings, fliers, and Internet postings and warned of the "wrath of God" descending to avenge these incidents." Klanwatch's chief investigator, Joe Roy, has warned that "the volatile combination of hate-filled rhetoric, paramilitary training, and heavy weaponry within the hard-core militia underground makes the likelihood of further violence very high." Although it would have been impossible to prevent the Oklahoma bombing, the FBI and other organizations may have been able to put out a threat advisory for federal facilities as they did after the event.

One challenge facing the FBI is conducting counterterrorist investigations and operations without violating the Constitution, as Hoover did liberally in the 1960s. When COINTELPRO came to public attention in 1972, Americans were shocked at how much the FBI had delved into private lives. Although COINTELPRO was successful and the FBI was doing exactly what the President requested, that success was won at the high cost of disregarding constitutional rights and even the lives of innocents. Today, United States Citizens are intolerant of such privacy invasions and, as Congress indicated, would never accept the expansion of FBI jurisdiction " In Israel and Great Britain. However, extended powers granted to law enforcement authorities seem to be welcomed.

The citizen's these countries have tacitly agreed that the primary concern is to get the terrorists and stop the slaughter by any means necessary, even if that means limited freedoms for them. As discussed in chapters three and four, most infringements of constitutional rights do not affect the general population. In England, the latest Prevention of Terrorism Act is directed solely at the perpetrators of the crime. An alleged terrorist can be convicted based on testimony by a suspect witness and/or detailed evidence Detention is allowable for up to seven days based on suspicion of law enforcement authorities. In court, a suspect can be tried without a jury. Although attempts have been made to inform the British public of these offenses to human rights, they seem satisfied with the proficiency of their law enforcement officials.

Israel has suspended rights for those Palestinians and Arabs living within their borders. Interrogation processes can be harsh, brutal, and sometimes deadly. Curfews are routinely ordered for Arab neighborhoods, and searches can be conducted without a warrant, often disrupting everyday life. The Israeli Jews do not protest these human rights violations since they are unaffected. Perhaps this is why right-wing groups have begun to come to the forefront. Both Israel and Great Britain have been under constant terrorist attacks. It seems that when these attacks happen with such frequency, people want results no matter the cost. They will give up democratic freedoms if it halts deadly terrorist activities.

SYMPATHY FOR THE DEVIL?

One of the makings of a successful terrorist or terrorist group is to gain sympathy and support from the population, no matter how severe the crime is. The usual object of a successful terrorist is to put the government in such a position to prove its ineffectiveness. This, in turn, causes the people to distrust the government in power and turn to the terrorists for answers and change. Once that occurs, the terrorists can have a measure of success, gaining their demands through the government's impotence. Because the population in the United States is ethnically mixed and most domestic terrorist groups are based on racism and bigotry, sympathy has never been a problem for the FBI. In the 1960s, with white and black hate groups, there might have been tacit support through money and rhetoric, but when it came down to the dirty work, such as bombing or murdering, only the most fanatical members could do it. Once a heinous deed has been committed by a group in the United States, it is like signing their own death warrant and waiting for the lynching party to appear. Although militia groups, hate groups, and pro-life groups work for change in the government, they do not have the overwhelming support of the people. Many Americans may grouse about the government but prefer change through the electoral process because it usually works.

In Great Britain, however, sympathy has been the determining factor in the success of the IRA and the British Army/RUC. When the IRA commits a deed, usually retaliatory, they are given whole-hearted approval by the Catholic population. IRA members can hide out for long periods in a sympathizer's house, and financing has never been a problem. They have even garnered sympathy and financing from supporters in the United States. On the other side, the British and Loyalists are just as sympathetic to the cause of Northern Ireland. Even with the cease-fire agreements and the Joint Declaration of Peace in effect, the British have clarified that if the IRA did not lay down their weapons before approaching the peace table, they were prepared to risk a resumption of violence. British Tory MP Sir Peter Temple-Morris stated in an interview with the Irish Republican News that "there is a willingness on this side of the water to tolerate, in certain circumstances, the thought of violence returning."

The Palestinians have always supported their terrorist groups, allowing them to hide in their houses or providing them with arms. Unfortunately for those terrorist groups, loyalty is almost non-existent, and sympathizers tire easily, especially if their livelihood is threatened. Eventually, the terrorists are on their own, which may be why they began to attack targets overseas. On the other side, the Israelis more or less supported their government, or at least they did until the peace initiatives went forward. Here they found themselves split, and some right-wing splinter groups took the anti-peace rhetoric seriously to the point of fanaticism. Unfortunately, the Israeli government was unaware of how serious they were until Yitzhak Rabin was assassinated Although sympathy may not bring down the government, it can bring about change. In Israel and Great Britain, peace was a long time coming because of sympathizers on both sides who were not willing to blink first. Perhaps the fact that elections and public opinion have, so far, brought about change when people are unhappy has been the reason why domestic terrorism fails to generate sympathy in the United States.

THE TERRORIST'S REASON FOR BEING

In the United States, those terrorists belonging to hate groups have an agenda based on some personal issue. They are racist, anti-Semitic, anti-gay or pro-life, and so on. The white supremacists believe that the existence of other races or ethnic groups on an equal level threatens their way of life. This is not about government control (except that some believe the government to be secretly run by Jews and that African Americans are their policemen) but a personal belief in their superiority based on history. Militia groups believe that constitutional rights are being eroded by laws made by the President and Congress. Gun control, civil rights, and legalized abortion are the government's way of controlling patriotic Americans and keeping them dependent. This belief is so deeply rooted that they disregard voting and the electoral process. Some militia groups have ties with white supremacists and the Ku Klux Klan. In Israel and Ireland, terrorists fight for land and religion for different reasons. Sinn Fein and the IRA believe Ireland should be united under a Catholic-influenced government. They resent that the British are assisting the Protestant citizens residing in Northern Ireland and suspect they have an ulterior motive (empire building). The Loyalist terrorists, on the other hand, believe that if Ireland is going to be united, the church and the government must remain separate and religious freedom allowed. They have decided that British rule and a continued connection to the Commonwealth will assure that, even if it means a divided Ireland.

Right-wing Israeli terrorists believe that the state of Israel and the occupied areas belong to them through their covenant with God. Muslims and Christians, although People of the Book, do not have that same covenant and are therefore not worthy of those privileges accorded to the Jews. Many are orthodox Jews and do not accept the laws governing the modern Jewish way of life. Although they were very active during the early days of Israel's independence, they went underground. They did not emerge terroristically until the 1990s when peace with the Palestinians became a reality. The Palestinians and their supporters believe that they were there first and that the region also has religious significance.

When the Arab-Israeli wars occurred, and the Israelis gained land, the Palestinians were told they were no longer welcome and became refugees. The PLO began fighting for the defeat of Zionism and recognition as people but could not field an army to defeat Israel. Therefore, the PLO used terrorism as a substitute for military aims. Israel and Great Britain have begun negotiations for peace, which suggests that the terrorists were partially successful. The government has recognized them, making them legitimate and elevating them to the international arena. The Palestinians have gained autonomy, but hard-core terrorists will settle for nothing less than obliterating the Israeli state from the face of the earth. The British and the Sinn Fein have yet to begin negotiations. White supremacists and militia groups in the United States are asking for changes such as repealing abortion and civil rights laws. The fundamental freedoms of others are at stake, and the FBI must ensure their protection as outlined in the Attorney General Guidelines.

POSSE COMITATUS

As discussed in chapters three and four, the fight against terrorism has fully involved the armies in both Israel and Great Britain. The *Shin Bet* and the IDF have an excellent, professional working relationship; they share intelligence information and frequently work together on counterterrorism operations. The military has the weapons and the equipment to get into places that the *Shin Bet* may not be able to penetrate. They also have commando units that can respond quickly when a terrorist situation escalates. The British Army was initially called in by Northern Ireland's government when the political crisis escalated to terroristic proportions. Although the RUC had dealt with small outbursts in the past, they were not prepared to face a well-armed IRA. Initially, when the Army arrived, they headed all the counterterrorist operations until the RUC protested. The British Army changed its operating procedures to technically assist the RUC. Unlike Israel's situation, too many organizations were involved in countering the ERA threat and were unwilling to work together. This created a confusing situation that inadvertently got men killed. In the United States, the Posse Comitatus Act passed one hundred seventeen years ago, sharply curtails the rights of the military to get involved in domestic law enforcement. This does not mean that the army has not been used in domestic law enforcement, as evidenced in chapter three, but for all intents and purposes, they do not and will not get involved. President Clinton's proposed Omnibus Counterterrorism Bill section offers what some congressmen consider a dangerous breach of the Posse Comitatus Act. The new law would permit the Attorney General, when investigating violations of the area, to request assistance "from any Federal, State, or local agency, including the Army, Navy and Air Force when biological and/or chemical terrorism is involved Senator Russ Feingold, D-Wisconsin, who voted against the Counterterrorism Bill, considers it "a vehicle to undo some of the traditional barriers which separate the federal government from state and local law enforcement."

David Kopel of the Independence Institute shares Feingold's misgivings about weakening the Posse Comitatus guidelines. While acknowledging that chemical or biological terrorism is not an impossibility, Kopel indicated that there are preemptive measures that are compatible with current guidelines:

> *"There are perfectly permissible ways for the military to share its expertise regarding chemical and biological terrorism with civilian law enforcement personnel. For example, it could train the FBI to deal with such threats, and the FBI could pass this along to local police. As long as the military is not actually enforcing civilian law, we can maintain the characteristics of a free society,"*

Israel and Great Britain do not have such limitations regarding their counterterrorist operations. In Israel, the military seems to be an advantage to the Shin Bet, but they appeared to be a hindrance in Northern Ireland. As a consideration for future counterterrorist operations in the United States, the military does not look like it will be participating in conjunction with the FBI due to heavy congressional opposition.

COUNTERTERRORISM IN THE UNITED STATES. THE FUTURE?

Israel and Great Britain have been battling terrorism for many years, and their governments have adjusted to get the better of terrorists and save lives. At times, both countries have been supremely successful, and in other operations have been tragic failures. No matter how long they have been at it, they have not found the absolute answer to deterring terrorism and protecting civilian targets. The FBI is entirely ruled by the Constitution and the Attorney General's guidelines. First and foremost, the victim's constitutional rights, pi the terrorist, must not be violated. Although they had significant successes with COINTELPRO, when it was discovered, the public did not remember those successes. They were appalled by the FBI's violation of democracy, the very democracy they were supposed to protect. The 1996 Summer Olympic Games will be held in Atlanta in July. Six million event tickets will be sold, and approximately 260,000 travelers will stay in the city. The 1972 Summer Olympics tragedy demonstrated the opportunity that a massive congregation of world-renowned athletes offered to terrorists, both domestic and international.

The FBI's involvement in the Summer Games stems from its mandate to counter the possibility that terrorists might view the Olympics as an appealing venue to execute a terrorist attack or stage an incident meant to attract international attention. In addition, historical, political, or longstanding ethnic rivalries among the fans, athletes, or officials of competing countries may also give way to terrorist acts of violence. The FBI may be challenged much more than during the 1984 Summer Olympics in Los Angeles Working closely with the Olympic security officials and numerous local, state, and federal law enforcement agencies, the FBI has headed the effort to form a coordinated counterterrorism network to neutralize any potential terrorist threat. Through a coordinated effort, security and terrorist concerns have been carefully scrutinized to preempt possible crisis situations. Only time will tell if those preparations are sufficient or even needed.

The FBI also investigates the industry's effort to combat terrorism through technology. For example, there is a move to incorporate taggants into explosives so that they will be easy to identify and track after a blast. Other innovations include nuclear quadrupole resonance, which scans for frequencies specific to explosives, and vapor detection methods, which examine and break down the vapor emanating from an explosive device. Many of these are being used separately or together in airports in Europe and the Middle East with excellent results. The Federal Aviation Administration, however, has strict guidelines for detection methods. Most are too expensive for industries to be willing to produce the technology. The FBI cannot wait for the United States to become a battleground for terrorists before it develops a counterterrorist plan The World Trade Center and the Oklahoma bombing have shown that, more than ever, they must be prepared and vigilant. It would be unrealistic to expect them to prevent all terrorist attacks, but that should be the goal. Working with other law enforcement and intelligence agencies should keep most terrorist attacks from being a surprise.

Milton Keynes UK
Ingram Content Group UK Ltd.
UKHW010627150124
436059UK00001B/169

9 798223 144151